PROFITS IN THE BRITISH ECONOMY 1909–1938

Institute of Economics and Statistics
Monograph No. 8

PROFITS IN THE
BRITISH ECONOMY
1909–1938

George David Norman *By*
G. D. N. WORSWICK *and* D. G. TIPPING

OXFORD
BASIL BLACKWELL
1967

© *Institute of Economics and Statistics, University of Oxford* 1967

The writers and the Oxford University Institute of Economics and Statistics, under whose auspices the research leading to the production of this book was carried out, wish to thank the Commissioners of Inland Revenue for their co-operation in making available the information and material relating to trade profits on which the book is based. The views expressed in the book, however, are those of the writers.

PRINTED IN GREAT BRITAIN
BY A. T. BROOME AND SON, 18 ST. CLEMENT'S, OXFORD
AND BOUND BY THE KEMP HALL BINDERY, OXFORD

FOREWORD

In 1949 the Commissioners of Inland Revenue offered to the Institute of Statistics access to statistical material concerning the trading profits of companies for various years from the turn of the century to the outbreak of the second World War. Mr. E. J. M. Buckatzsch was appointed Senior Research Officer of the Institute to undertake the enquiry. In the following years he did a great deal of work, assisted to begin with by Mr. C. R. Ross, examining the material in great detail and following up various problems arising from it, e.g. how far the data might be linked up with other data, such as output and employment, from the Census of Production. John Buckatzsch died in August 1954 before he could complete the study.

I undertook to pick up the threads of the work, and in 1958 Mr. David Tipping was appointed to the Institute to assist me. In the event we have re-worked all the statistics presented here from the original data provided by Inland Revenue. In its general outline the report follows Buckatzsch's original plan: and in the opening chapter we have followed fairly closely his draft. I had many conversations with Buckatzsch when he was working on this enquiry. He was most anxious that users of any statistics which he published should not put upon them a greater weight of inference than was justified by their nature. Mr. Tipping and I have endeavoured to respect his warning in such conclusions as we have drawn.

In one sense this report has been wholly done by Mr. Tipping and myself: but it owes its inspiration to John Buckatzsch, and we hope we have produced it in a form he would have found acceptable.

All of us at the Institute of Statistics who have worked on this material have received valuable help from various members of the Inland Revenue, in explaining how the figures were obtained, and answering all kinds of queries. The report has been submitted to their scrutiny, and with their help we believe we have produced a correct description of the data published here. Questions of economic interpretation and of opinion are entirely the responsibility of Mr. Tipping and myself.

G.D.N.W.

MONOGRAPHS OF THE OXFORD UNIVERSITY INSTITUTE OF ECONOMICS AND STATISTICS

CONTENTS

CHAPTER I

DESCRIPTION OF THE MATERIAL

The main tables of this report consist of classifications of the income liable to Income Tax under Schedule D, in certain years, according to the branch of economic activity to which the income accrued. The concepts of income on which the tables are based do not correspond exactly with any generally accepted economic category of income. Broadly speaking, however, the definition of income for Schedule D purposes leads to at least two income concepts which correspond fairly closely with concepts of 'profits' used in social accounting. Accordingly, our main tables may be regarded, with reservation, as a trade and industry analysis of the profits accruing outside agriculture in the British economy in certain years before the Second World War.

No such analysis has yet been published for years before 1937–8. The 92nd Report of the Commissioners of Inland Revenue[1] contained a trade classification of assessments made for 1937–8, 1938–9 and 1939–40, together with those made in 1948–9. Subsequent Reports contain a trade classification of assessments made each year. For earlier years, only the total 'True Income' corresponding to the gross assessments made in each year were published in the Board's Annual Reports. These estimates of total 'True Income' have provided the main source of information about trading profits in the British economy. In addition, the Reports contained a limited amount of information about the 'industrial' origin of the *gross assessments*. Down to the end of the First World War, the Reports showed separately the gross assessments made on enterprises in about half a dozen trade groups. These groups had been transferred to Schedule D from Schedule A in 1865–6. They included railways, mines, some types of ironworks, gasworks, cemeteries and salt springs, but no major manufacturing industry.[2] For later years, the Reports classify the gross assessments made under Schedule D in six very broad groups, including Manufacturing, Production and Mining; Distribution, Transport and Communication; Finance and Professions; and some categories of income from overseas.[3] The

[1] 92nd Report of the Commissioners of His Majesty's Inland Revenue, London, Oct. 1950, Tables 40–79.
[2] See e.g. 59th Report, Table 54.
[3] See e.g. 77th Report, Table 49.

adjustments (for 'Other Reductions and Discharges' and 'Wear and Tear') by which the gross assessments can be converted into estimates of 'True Income' are, however, not classified. Consequently, on the basis of the information hitherto published, the total 'True Income' assessed in years before 1937–8 cannot be allocated even to the half dozen broad categories into which the gross assessments made in those years are classified.

With the use of data which the Board of Inland Revenue has now made available, it has been possible to allocate all 'True Income' to the branch of activity in which it originated. About one hundred trade groups have been distinguished, covering all enterprises engaged in extraction, manufacturing, distribution, transport, finance and the professions, and enterprises domiciled in the U.K. but operating overseas. The results are given in the main tables of this report. Apart from differences in classification, our tables represent a backward projection into the inter-war period and beyond, of the trade and industry tables from 1937–8 and later years published by the Board.

In addition to a trade and industry analysis of 'True Income' as defined for Schedule D purposes, our tables include estimates of the number of enterprises in the various trade groups in the years in question. The enterprises are, moreover, classified according to their institutional type. Two types of enterprise are distinguished—non-corporate, i.e. individuals and 'firms' or private partnerships, and corporate, i.e. companies and other enterprises, such as local authorities and trade associations. Our tables therefore throw some light on changes in the institutional form of ownership in the business enterprise sector of the economy since before the First World War.

It will be seen that our main tables relate to six years before the Second World War. Strictly speaking, they relate to assessments made in the years 1911–12, 1928–29 and 1933–34, and to assessments made for 1937–38, 1938–39 and 1939–40. The time-reference of the estimates of 'True Income' corresponding to these assessments cannot be exactly defined in terms of calendar years. Broadly speaking, the assessments made in 1911–12 relate to incomes which accrued in the calendar years 1908, 1909 and 1910, the assessment being based, as far as most enterprises were concerned, on an average of the 'profits' of those three years. The assessments made in 1928–29 and 1933–34 of the series represent (again speaking generally) 'True Income' which accrued in the preceding year, the 'moving average' basis of assessment having been abandoned in 1927. The columns of our tables are headed '1909',

'1927', '1932', '1936', '1937', and '1938' because for many purposes this has seemed the least misleading way of describing the time-reference of our figures as estimates of 'profits' accruing. It must however be emphasised that for reasons to be explained our figures cannot be exactly related to any given calendar year. It is convenient and, up to a point, justifiable to regard our tables as 'trade and industry analyses of the profits accruing in given years'. Strictly speaking, however, they are estimates of the income, as defined for Schedule D purposes, corresponding to assessments made in or for certain years.

It is not possible to construct tables similar to our main tables for years other than those to which our tables refer. The necessary data for such tables are not available. The gross and net *assessments* made in two other years, 1890–91 and 1895–96, were classified by the Inland Revenue authorities, but it is not possible to derive estimates of the 'True Income' corresponding to these assessments. Some useful information has been derived from these early 'Trade Classifications', however, and is included in Appendix D.

THE CONCEPT OF TRUE INCOME

The Schedule D statistics include, or imply, statements of at least three concepts of income: the 'Gross Income' assessed in a given year; the 'True Income' corresponding to that Gross Income; and the 'Actual Income' on which income tax is paid. The relationship between these three concepts is explicitly shown in most Annual Reports of the Inland Revenue.[1]

Of these concepts, True Income is the one of greatest general interest. True Income represents income which is deemed to have actually accrued to enterprises. Gross Income describes rather the result of administrative activity and Actual Income measures a quantity of essentially fiscal interest. The 'analysis of trading profits by trade groups' in the 92nd and subsequent Reports of Inland Revenue is in fact an analysis of True Income, and the same is true of the analysis of earlier years presented in the present report.

The concept of True Income is not explicitly used in the Annual Reports for inter-war years. It has, however, been possible to derive estimates of the True Income assessed in those years from information given in some of the Tables in the earlier reports.[2] As the more recent

[1] See e.g. Table 39 of the 92nd Report (Assessments made in 1948–9).
[2] See e.g. Table 55 of the 73rd Report (Assessments made in 1938–9).

Reports show explicitly, True Income is obtained by deducting various items from Gross Income assessed. These items fall into three main categories. The first consists of essentially notional items, resulting partly from the administrative procedure of making partly arbitrary preliminary assessments. These items make up the 'Overcharges' shown in Table 39 of the 92nd Report and corresponding tables in later Reports. The second group of adjustments made to Gross Income are those made on account of Trading Losses and related matters. The third group consists of deductions on account of certain types of expenses not treated elsewhere. In the tables given in Annual Reports for inter-war years, such as Table 55 of the 73rd Report, all these items are combined under the heading 'Other Reductions and Discharges'.

Subtraction of the 'Adjustments' shown in the recent Reports, or the 'Other Reductions and Discharges' of the earlier series, from Gross Income assessed leads to a statement of True Income *gross* of Wear and Tear allowances made by the authorities. This quantity is referred to in the recent Reports as 'Gross True Income'. Both the more recent and the earlier series of Annual Reports show separately the Wear and Tear allowances (referred to as 'Depreciation Allowances', then as 'Capital Allowances' in the later Reports) made against Gross True Income. The deduction of these allowances leads to a statement of 'Net True Income' in the later Reports. Finally the deduction of various 'Exemptions' leads to a statement of 'Actual Income'. The exemptions fall into two principal categories, namely incomes below the current exemption limit in so far as they 'come under the purview of the Department', and that part of incomes assessed under Schedule D which is paid out to charities and is therefore free of tax.

In order to construct the main tables of this report it has been necessary to make similar deductions from the Gross Income assessed on each of the various trade groups. Unpublished trade classifications of Gross Income assessed in 1911-2, 1928-9 and 1933-4 existed, and of the Wear and Tear allowed when the assessments were made; this data provided the basis of the final estimates of True Income.[1] The Gross Income assessed on any trade group and the 'Adjustments'[2] necessary to reduce it to the Gross True Income of the group are of purely technical interest and are not included in our main tables. The Wear and Tear allowances made to enterprises in the various trade

[1] The estimates for 1936, 1937 and 1938 are based on the results of a direct sampling investigation made by the Inland Revenue Authorities. See p. (5).

[2] I.e. the 'Other Reductions and Discharges' in the terminology of the inter-war Annual Reports.

groups, however, are of some general interest and have been shown separately in the main tables. The Net True Income of each group, determined by deducting the group's wear and tear allowance from its Gross True Income, is also shown. On the other hand, it is not possible to allocate the 'Exemptions' among the various trade groups. For this reason it is not possible to make a trade classification of 'Actual Income'.[1]

In attempting to arrive at a trade classification of True Income from the Gross Income assessed in 1911–2 it was found necessary to use estimates of some of the adjusted items. It was also found necessary to amalgamate some of the trade groups in order to reduce the possible errors involved in the use of these estimates. Both the Gross and Net True Income and the Wear and Tear Allowances shown for the various trade groups for the assessment year 1911–2 are estimates of the 'true figures' but it is believed that they are trustworthy estimates.

'Correct' accounting figures were available for most of the 'Other Reductions and Discharges' in each trade group for the assessments made in 1928–9 and 1933–4. Part of the total adjustment in each trade group however had to be estimated, but the amounts involved were relatively small. The allocation of the amounts was made on the basis of an indicator considered satisfactory by experts in this field. The Wear and Tear allowances against the Gross True Income assessed in these years on each trade group were, so far as they were allowed at the time of assessment and not by a consequent adjustment, exactly known as accounting quantities. Accordingly the figures given in our tables for Gross and Net True Income assessed in 1928–9 and 1933–4 may be accepted as close estimates of the 'correct' Schedule D quantities.

The figures shown in the tables for the True Income assessed for the years 1937–38, 1938–39 and 1939–40 were arrived at by wholly different methods. They were obtained by sampling the finally agreed (i.e. 'adjusted') assessments for these years in each trade group. The samples included 20 per cent of the assessments and were controlled

---

[1] In any case, even if it could be made, a classification of Actual Income would be of somewhat limited interest. For in estimating it, allowance has been made for certain categories of income which accrued to enterprises in the first place but was passed on by way of dividend, etc., to persons or bodies exempt from Income Tax. Incomes received by Charities, amounting to £20 m. annually in the inter-war years, were the most important of these exempt categories, though it should be noted that most of these incomes were dividends received by charities from companies not themselves exempt. The difference between *total* Net True Income and Actual Income was about £30 m. in the years covered by our tables.

at certain stages. This sampling method also provided the basis of the trade classification for those years published in the 92nd Report.

The figures for these three years shown in our main tables and those given in the 92nd Report have a common origin in the 20 per cent sample; but they are not comparable. Apart from differences in the trade classifications and certain differences in coverage, the 92nd Report figures have been processed one stage further than ours. The authors of the 92nd Report considered that the 196–6 forms (statements of liability in the case of profits over £2,000) gave a better indication of the trend of profits from year to year then the 'over £2,000' cases in the sample. The latter were therefore aggregated over the three years and redistributed in proportion to the 196–6 totals. For the 'under £2,000' cases the sample figures were used.

The same process could have been performed on our figures, but the advantages would have been doubtful. In the first place, the set of 196–6 forms was not complete and in some trade groups may have constituted a biased sample. By combining trade groups, as was done in the 92nd Report, this objection could be overcome, but at the expense of a loss in detail. In this study, 94 trade groups are distinguished, as opposed to 38 in the 92nd Report. In the second place, the sample figures are considered to give a better indication of the size of profits, and therefore of the relative importance of the various trade groups in the total of any one year. If the accuracy of our measure of trend were to have been improved by this use of 196–6 data, it might have been at the expense of the accuracy of our measure of the distribution of profits.

The overall effect of this adjustment to the trend of profits is anyway not very great, although for certain trade groups it may be more marked. The difference between the totals in the 92nd Report[1] and the Grand Totals of Gross True Income in our main tables is shown below.

	1936	1937	1938	3-year total
92nd Report (£m)	1,117	1,195	1,118	3,430
Index No. (1937=100) ..	93.5	100.0	93.6	
Grand Total (£m)	1,096	1,161	1,065	3,322
Index No. (1937=100)	94.4	100.0	91.8	

Whichever estimate of the trend one takes, it can only be an approximation. This must also be remembered when interpreting the figures of profit estimated for the individual trade groups. Being based on a sample, they may not be as accurate as those for 1927 and 1932.

[1] Table 40, p. 57.

From what has been said it will be clear that while all the figures in our main tables are to some extent based on estimates, the results may be accepted as good approximations to the 'correct' figures of the income on which enterprises in each trade group were deemed liable to taxation (before or after deduction of depreciation allowances) under Schedule D. In other words, the figures in the tables are estimates of certain fixed quantities, defined by the current Income Tax Acts.

INTERPRETATION OF THE DATA.

It is now necessary to consider how far the 'correct' figures to which we offer approximations would be economically meaningful. In particular, it is necessary to decide how closely Gross True Income corresponds with trading profits before deducting sums set aside to make good depreciation and similar capital charges; how closely the Wear and Tear allowances correspond with sums actually set aside for this purpose; and thus how far the resulting Net True Income figures provide a good estimate of net trading profits.

These questions were exhaustively discussed by Stamp[1] among others. It is unnecessary to repeat Stamp's arguments. In general he concluded that in spite of the formidable list of theoretical divergences between the quantity defined as True Income for Schedule D purposes and trading profits in the ordinary sense, the quantitative difference was very small in practice. It must be remembered, however, that Stamp was considering the *whole* of the income assessed under Schedule D and he relies at several points on the proposition that what may be true of the parts (namely that the quantities defined by the fiscal and the accounting definitions of profits may differ significantly) is not necessarily true of the whole. In other words, Stamp seems to have relied on various components of difference cancelling each other. It is not certain that he would have done so if he had been dealing with specific trade groups, or with a period marked by acute economic flutuations as we are here.

Several aspects of the definition of True Income must be borne in mind when the figures are interpreted as estimates of profits in the accounting sense. In the first place, the concept of profits for Schedule D purposes includes some items and excludes others which would probably be respectively excluded and included by a conventional definition of trading profits. The schema below sets out a comparison

[1] See *British Incomes and Property*, Chapter VI.

of those items which are included in the Schedule D assessment and those which are excluded.

Included	Excluded
1. Remuneration of proprietors in non-corporate enterprises.	7. Directors' fees and salaries.
2. Patent royalties.	8. Profits tax.
3. Long lease rents.	9. Schedule A rental value of land and buildings.
4. Debenture interest.	10. Other interest charges.
5. Dividend distributions.	11. Non-trading income.
6. Undistributed profits.	

In the case of firms and partnerships economic theory would demand the exclusion of item 1 from the calculation of profit, so as to make it comparable with corporate profits from which item 7 has been excluded. In practice it is not feasible to estimate the wage or salary element in the income of sole traders and partnerships. Nor is it necessary for the tax authorities to attempt this, since the income would be taxable however defined.

Items 2 and 3 could also be regarded technically as costs of production. Both represent payments to factors which have been hired or rented, as opposed to distributions of profit among 'entrepreneurs'. (An exception would be in the case of royalties paid as a proportion of profits, the patent constituting a form of equity). Rents and fixed royalties must be paid regardless of profit or loss. However, for administrative purposes income from these items is taxed at source.

If item 3 is included one would expect item 9 to be included also. The rental value of owner-occupied land and buildings is included as part of profit for National Income accounting purposes, but this is done by adding together the separate Schedule A and D quantities. The figures in this report refer only to Schedule D quantities.

Item 4 is traditionally regarded in economic theory as a deductible cost, being payment to non-entrepreneurial factors. Apart from the administrative reason for including it so that tax may be deducted at source, there is theoretical justification for including it. To get comparative results of trading activity in different trades, the figures of trading profit should not distinguish between those trades in which a greater or lesser amount of capital was raised by debenture as opposed to equity issues. (To be consistent, all income earned on long term loans should be included, such as interest paid on a mortgage.)

Non-trading income is rightly excluded, as not being directly related to current trading activity. In those cases where such income arises from shareholdings in other enterprises, tax will be deducted at source and the corresponding income included in the total for that source.

Finally, the exclusion of profits tax, item 8, is due to fiscal policy. This is a payment out of income and might therefore be included. In fact, this tax applied only from April 1st, 1937, and then at a maximum rate of 5 per cent. Our results are therefore barely affected. (Since 1952 profits tax has not been deducted).

Another difficulty in the interpretation of True Income arises from the treatment of trading losses by the Inland Revenue. This may have considerable, but not exactly definable, effects on the amount of True Income assessed in any given year. These effects may arise in three ways.

(i) Since 1927, as a substitute for including losses in a three-year average, losses made by an enterprise in any given year may be carried forward and offset against profits made by the enterprise in any of the six following years, and in some circumstances, still later.

(ii) Under the Income Tax Act of 1918, a loss may be allowed against the *statutory* income of the year, e.g. an amount based on the previous year's profit, or income taxed by deduction in the current year.

The consequences of these two effects are important. Unless the losses carried forward out of any given assessment year equal those brought forward *into* it, the True Income assessed in that year will either exceed or fall short of the True Income actually accruing in the period corresponding to the assessment year. Under the conditions experienced in the inter-war period, it can hardly be assumed that, in all trade groups, treatment of losses by the Inland Revenue authorities had no effect on estimates of True Income. Indeed in some trade groups we should expect, on the contrary, that the figures would be appreciably affected. In particular, the apparent True Income of some trade groups would be reduced in years *following* a year in which heavy losses had been sustained. The figures for cotton and shipbuilding may have been affected in this way in the period covered by the assessments made in 1933–4.[1] The effect of the 'loss' provisions of the Income Tax Acts is therefore to give rise to a possible divergence between the figures in the tables and the profits actually accruing to enterprises in the corresponding years. There is however no means of measuring the amounts of such divergencies nor, consequently, of correcting for them.

[1] At first sight the same might appear to be true of 1911–2 but at that time losses were not carried forward but came into the 3-year average.

B

Not only may the figures for total True Income be affected by the 'loss' provisions, but also the number of assessments made in any one year, since enterprises making net losses will not appear in the assessments.

(iii) The authorities allow losses made by one enterprise in a given year to be offset against the profits made in that year by another enterprise under the same ownership. If the two enterprises were mainly engaged in different production activities, this rule might cause a transfer of True Income between the two trade groups. It is thought, however, that the amounts of such transfers would be too small to exercise a significant effect upon the True Income figures for the various trade groups.

When we come to interpret the figures of *Net* True Income a further difficulty arises from uncertainty as to the economic significance of the sums granted as Wear and Tear allowances. The temptation is to regard these sums as representing fairly accurately the sums set aside by industry to meet depreciation and similar capital charges. If it were permissible to do this, the Wear and Tear allowances would introduce no *new* element of uncertainty into the True Income figures. In practice, however, the allowances bear an uncertain relationship to the sums actually set aside to meet depreciation, and the figures for Net True Income are affected by this uncertainty.

'The allowances are computed on the basis prescribed by Statute. They may or may not correspond with the amounts deducted by the trader in his own accounts.'[1] The extent of the probable divergence between the statutory allowance and the deductions actually made is no doubt greater when replacement costs are rapidly and continuously rising than at other times. The actual divergence may have been smaller in the inter-war years than it has been at certain times since then. There is yet a third method of measuring depreciation, namely the attempt to estimate the 'true' capital consumption at current replacement costs of all fixed assets, independently of actual accounting practice. The complete scepticism about the significance of the statutory allowances in post-war years led the authors of the National Income Blue Books to abandon the attempt to estimate National Income net of depreciation, but estimates of capital consumption are now given in their place. Comparison of these figures with those for depreciation allowances suggests a wide divergence in the early nineteen-fifties, even allowing for the wider coverage of the former.

[1] 92nd Annual Report, section 93, p. 55.

The greater use of investment and initial allowances since then, and the larger proportion of assets which have been installed at recent prices, have now led to a greatly reduced gap between these two measures, and presumably between either of these two measures and the sums actually set aside by enterprises. As to the inter-war period, with the statutory allowances becoming progressively more generous, and prices at times changing quite considerably, little can be said with certainty.

The Wear and Tear allowances were no doubt originally intended to be realistic, and to make possible the accumulation of adequate sums to cover depreciation during the probable life of the equipment concerned. Nevertheless, an exact correspondence in any given year between the Wear and Tear allowances made to any given trade group and sums actually set aside by the enterprises in that group must have been a coincidence, and could not have been predicted.

In the first place a considerable amount of the actual depreciation was met by allowances for repairs and renewals made in the process of arriving at Gross True Income. The greater part of the depreciation of gasworks and railways, for example, was dealt with in this way. It will be noticed that the Wear and Tear allowances made to enterprises in these groups are a very small proportion of Gross True Income. Allowances under Schedule D for depreciation of buildings was confined to mills and factories. No allowances for depreciation are made under Schedule A, which provides only for repairs, insurance and management. It was estimated in 1930 that the written-down value of plant and machinery[1] on which repairs and renewals were being allowed instead of Wear and Tear was as follows:

	£mn.
British railways	132
Foreign railways	66
Gasworks in the U.K.	50
Waterworks in the U.K.	65
Coal and iron works	20
Other manufacturing	20
Transport and distribution	20
Concerns operating abroad (other than railways) ...	10
Total	383

[1] Not buildings.

These estimates were based on a sample of original returns and balance sheet values. The U.K. railways remained on the renewals basis until 1938. The L.P.T.B. was dealt with on the Wear and Tear basis from its inception in 1933, because it included road undertakings as well as railways. In the iron industry, furnace structures were dealt with on the renewals basis to 1938–9, and on the Wear and Tear basis in 1939–40. Overall, the field of repairs and renewals is greater the further back one goes.

In the second place, the Wear and Tear allowances made in any given assessment year included sums carried forward from earlier years. For it was provided that if the Gross Income accruing to an enterprise in a given year were *less* than the Wear and Tear allowance 'normally' claimed by it, the balance of the allowance could be carried forward and set against the profits of later years.

Finally, the whole structure of the allowances (as distinct from those in respect of repairs and renewals) was based on assumptions about the average lives of different types of equipment. These assumptions may have been justified, taking one year with another and over the whole of manufacturing industry, as Stamp seems to have been prepared to believe.[1] But it is unlikely that actual depreciation, in any given trade group, corresponded closely year by year to the sums allowed by the authorities for Wear and Tear. The allowances made were increased from time to time. The 1932 Income Tax Act granted an 'additional allowance' of one-tenth of the normal allowance. In 1935 an official instruction accepted a ruling by the appeal Commissioners that the 'additional allowance' need not be deducted in computing the written-down value on which the next allowance would be given. (It was, however, to be taken into account on any obsolescence claim.) In 1938, the 'additional allowance' was increased to one-fifth of the normal allowance.

These considerations obviously affect the significance of the figures for Net True Income arrived at by deducting the Wear and Tear allowances from computed Gross True Income. But it is not possible to estimate the extent of the effect. In principle, Gross True Income as the fiscal counterpart of gross trading profits is a less interesting quantity than Net True Income, the fiscal counterpart of net trading profits after meeting depreciation. In practice, however, it appears that Gross True Income may well correspond more closely with gross trading profits than Net True Income does with net trading profits,

[1] *British Incomes and Property*, p. 196.

and in this sense may be a more useful quantity in economic investigations.

Certain administrative factors affecting the scope of the Schedule D figures from time to time must also be mentioned. First there is the geographical coverage. After the First World War, that part of Ireland which became Eire was excluded from the coverage of the figures. The proportion of True Income assessed in 1911–12 which can be attributed to Eire was between one and two per cent. In some trades, e.g. brewing, it may have been more. Such a small difference can be regarded as falling within the range of uncertainty attaching to the estimate of True Income assessed in 1911–12.

The other important administrative factor concerns the exemption limit. In general, the figures relate to the total of incomes above the current exemption limit, although this is not strictly true in practice of the figures given in our tables for True Income assessed in 1911–12, 1928–29 and 1933–34. In all these years the figures include small sums made up of incomes below the exemption limit. This applies only to non-corporate enterprises; there is no exemption limit for corporate concerns. In the years 1928–29 and 1933–34, the total of incomes included from below the exemption limit was about £20 m. Such incomes would be included because other sources of income would raise them over the exemption limit; to keep them in the record on the chance of higher incomes being earned in subsequent years; or because a first estimate suggested a possible tax liability.

In principle it would be desirable to add to the True Income of each trade group the appropriate amount of income below the exemption limit. The amount of such income, over and above the £20 m. already included would, however, be very small in the inter-war period.

The exemption limit was £160 in 1911–2, £162 in 1928–9 and £125 in 1933–4, and from 1937–8 to 1939–40. The small change in the nominal exemption limit between 1911–2 and 1928–9 is somewhat misleading, unless the change in the general price-level between these years is remembered.[1] If the general price-level be supposed to have

[1] The following price indices, taken from the *London and Cambridge Bulletin*, give an indication of price movements during the years covered in this report.

			Retail prices	Wholesale prices	
				Manufactures	Basic Materials
1913	..	..	64	83	96
1927	..	..	107	117	134
1932	..	..	92	84	84
1936	..	..	94	93	98
1937	..	..	99	107	115
1938	..	..	100	100	100

risen by 50 per cent between the two years, the nominal exemption limit of 1911–2 would be equivalent to one of £240 in 1928–9. In other words the effective exemption limit was considerably lower in 1928–9 than it had been in 1911–2. In comparison the change in the *nominal* exemption limit between 1928–9 and 1933–4 may have been much smaller in real terms. Indeed, the price change between these years may have implied a raising of the *effective* limit between 1928–9 and 1933–4. The effect of these changes on the scope of the Schedule D statistics can have been important only in those trade groups in which a significant proportion of the total True Income accrued to very small enterprises. This means in effect trade groups like the Distributive trades and the Building trades. Even here, however, the effect was probably greater as between 1911–2 and 1928–9 than between 1928–9 and any later years. The effect on the number of assessments made would probably be greater than the effect on the amount of True Income assessed.

SUMMARY. The following points must be borne in mind in interpreting statements of the True Income of trade groups assessed in any given year.

1. The definition of trading profits for the computation of Schedule D liability excludes certain items included in the normal definition of trading profits, and includes certain items normally excluded. This affects the scope of both Gross and Net True Income to the degree to which these concepts do not correspond respectively with gross and net trading profits in the ordinary sense.

2. The treatment of trading losses may have an important effect on both the Gross and Net True Income shown for any given trade group. True Income may be transferred, as a result of the loss provisions, between years and between trade groups.

3. The sums allowed for Wear and Tear in any given assessment year may or may not correspond closely with the sums actually set aside for depreciation in the corresponding accounting years. This affects the degree to which Net True Income corresponds with net trading profits in the ordinary sense of the term.

4. Administrative changes in the exemption limit (particularly when price changes are taken into account) and in the types of income assessable under Schedule D affect the strict comparability of figures for True Income in different years. These effects are in fact not likely to be large in practice and are confined mainly to certain trade groups.

Finally, no attempt has been made to estimate the possible extent of evasion of Income Tax liability. Attempts have been made by other writers to estimate the effect of evasion on the *total* True Income assessed in various years. There is, however, no obvious way of making such estimates for separate trade groups. To the extent that evasion occurred, our figures are under-statements of the taxable True Income which actually accrued.

THE TIME-REFERENCE OF THE ESTIMATES OF TRUE INCOME.

The estimates of True Income in the tables are based on Schedule D assessments made *in* 1911–2, 1928–9 and 1933–4, and on assessments made *for* 1937–8, 1938–9 and 1939–40. For many purposes it is necessary to know fairly precisely the period of time in which the corresponding True Income accrued. In fact it is not possible to define this period exactly.

Two technical points must first be mentioned. The first concerns the distinction between assessments made *in* a given year and assessments *for* a given year. The second point concerns the theoretical basis of the assessments made in the various years of our series.

In principle, the assessments made *for* a given year relate to the income which accrued in the corresponding accounting period (whatever that may have been), irrespective of the year in which this income was actually assessed. In practice, a concern's assessment might not be finally agreed until some years after the assessment year in which it would normally have been made. Thus the assessments made *in* any given year consist mainly of assessments *for* that year, but

(i) exclude assessments carried forward to later years, and

(ii) include assessments brought forward from previous years. Strictly speaking, the economist is interested in the True Income corresponding to assessments made *for* any given year, rather than the income assessed *in* that year. However, as far as the total gross assessment is concerned the difference between the assessments made *in* 1928–9 and 1933–4 and the assessments made *for* these years was probably small. In Appendix B the gross assessments made in the years 1926–7 to 1939–40 are analysed into assessments in respect of current and previous years. It will be seen that about 93 per cent of the gross assessments made in both 1928–9 and 1933–4 consisted of assessments made *for* these years. In each year assessments carried forward from the previous year were nearly equal to assessments carried forward to the next year; about half the assessments carried forward came from the previous year and the remaining half from earlier years. It must be remembered that these figures relate to gross assessments, not to True Income; and that they relate to the whole of Schedule D including the Interest and other items not classified in our main tables. Nothing is known of the distribution of these 'transferred' assessments among trade groups, although it is supposed that most of them related to individuals and partnerships. Assessments on trade groups in which these preponderated would therefore be more affected than assessments on the more corporately organised trades.

The second point concerns the basis of the assessments made for the various years covered by our tables. The assessments made in 1911–2 are based in principle (i.e. in so far as they are equivalent to assessments made *for* 1911–2) on the average income of a varying number of preceding years. Most concerns, including those engaged in manufacturing, distribution and commerce, were assessed on the average income of three years preceding the year of assessment. The assessments on such concerns made up about 72 per cent of the gross assessments made in 1908–9. Mines, accounting for about 3 per cent of the whole assessment, were assessed on the average of the five preceding years, railways and gasworks (12 per cent) on the year immediately preceding, and certain interest and income from abroad (13 per cent) on the actual year itself. Broadly speaking, therefore, the True Income assessed in 1911–2 in the various trade groups represented averages of the incomes of recent years. It did not *in principle* relate to the actual income of any one year except in the case of gasworks, railways and the special categories of income and interest from abroad.

Since the assessments in 1911–2 were averages of incomes for one, three, or five preceding years (according to the trade group), estimates of True Income cannot, except by accident, represent the profits accruing in any actual calendar year. They represent rather a kind of 'average' state of affairs existing about 1909, reflecting the changing state of trade during the period 1908–10. We shall *describe* them as profits of 1909.[1]

The assessments made in 1928–9 and 1933–4 were, again in principle, normally based on the 'Schedule D income' which accrued in the preceding year. This was interpreted as the income which accrued to each enterprise in the accounting year ending during the year preceding the assessment year. The assessments made in 1928–9 should therefore relate to the income accruing to enterprises in accounting years ending

[1] Stamp, J., *British Incomes and Property*, p. 177, note 2.

between April 1927 and April 1928. This income may have actually accrued in any period of up to one year between April 1926 and April 1928. It is however impossible to estimate the proportion of the *total* income accruing to all enterprises in that period which came to be assessed in 1928–9, and how much had been assessed in 1927–8, for the accounting years of the various enterprises must have overlapped each other. In some groups, such as the professions, and in others in which assessments on 'Individuals' were predominant, the modal accounting year may have coincided fairly closely with the year preceding the assessment year (i.e. for 1928–9, with the financial year April 1927 to April 1928). But in other groups it may have differed very appreciably. In general, it may be supposed that the income assessed in 1928–9 represents roughly income accruing in 1927, while that assessed in 1933–4 represents roughly income accruing in 1932.

The figures representing True Income for the last three years given in our main tables are not based on assessments made *in* the corresponding years. They are based on samples drawn from the assessment made *for* the years in question. They therefore represent the greater part of the 'profits' accruing in the Income Tax years 1937–8, 1938–9 and 1939–40. They may be taken to represent roughly the profits accruing in 1936, 1937 and 1938 respectively.[1]

The time-reference of the estimates of True Income is also affected, as already mentioned, by the carrying forward of losses or depreciation allowances from earlier years. The effects of this would be particularly marked in years following severe depression in any trade group.

In spite of the impossibility of identifying the True Income *assessed* in any year with the accounting profits *accruing* in any calendar year, we have adopted a convention of referring to 'True Income assessed in 1928–9' as 'True Income of 1927' and so on. Provided the considerations mentioned in the preceding paragraphs are borne in mind, this convention has considerable advantages over the technically more correct definition of the estimates. In the first place, it enables us to avoid endless repetition of the words 'assessed in' in reference to the estimates in discussing our results. In the second place, our convention seems more natural than the technically correct definition. For the main object of the present publication is to provide material for studies of the economic history of the inter-war period, and in such studies the estimates of True Income will almost inevitably be used as approximate estimates of profits accruing in calendar years. Indeed, it is difficult to

[1] 92nd Annual Report, para. 92, p. 55.

see how our results can be used by economists in any other way. At the same time, anyone using our results in this way must bear in mind the inexactness of the implied time-references. Strictly speaking, estimates of True Income derived from assessments made under Schedule D can have *no* exact time-reference in terms of calendar years. Accordingly, such estimates are not directly comparable with any other quantities, such as estimates of output and employment, which may relate to definite calendar years.

THE TRADE CLASSIFICATION.

The True Income classified in our main tables consists of that part of the True Income assessed under Schedule D which arose from trading or 'productive' enterprise in a broad sense. Some categories of income assessed under Schedule D, consisting mainly of various types of interest, are not classified in the main tables.

The basis of classification followed in the main tables is that adopted by the Inland Revenue authorities for their classifications of gross assessments from 1911–12 to 1933–34 and of final assessments from 1937–38 to 1939–40. The starting-point of the study was, as already observed, a series of already existing classifications of assessments, and not the original mass of assessments. In this sense the hundred odd trade-groups distinguished in the Inland Revenue authorities' classifications of assessments are ultimate units for the present study. The trade groups can be combined in various ways, but they cannot be further sub-divided. The main tables therefore preserve the trade-group structure of the original classifications of assessments, though for purposes of analysis and discussion the groups have been combined and grouped together in various ways.

Ideally, tables like the main tables of this report would show the True Income accruing from each of a number of specified productive activities. More specifically, the income shown for any activity would (*a*) arise from that activity alone, and (*b*) represent the whole of the income arising from that activity. The classification of productive activities might be made on any one of a large number of sets of criteria. For many purposes it would probably be useful to distinguish major branches of productive activity, such as manufacturing, distribution, transport and so on, and within each of these branches, to distinguish types of activity, generally according to the types of material used. Thus manufacturing activity would be sub-divided into textile trades, metal trades and so on, and each of these further sub-divided into the cotton trade, the linen trade and so on. The strict logic of such a classification is perhaps difficult to establish, but its utility has been established in practice. Most trade and industry classifications of employment and output are of this kind in principle, though they vary in the degree to which homogeneity and mutual exclusiveness of the classes have been achieved. In practice, it just is not possible to give a breakdown of profits in this manner.

The classification of True Income in this report falls short of the ideal standard that has been proposed. The reason for this is that the basis of the classification is a classification of enterprises, any of which may have been engaged in more than one type or even branch of productive activity. Multiple enterprises of this kind have been allocated to trade-groups according to the type of activity in which they were 'mainly engaged'. It is not possible to sub-divide the True Income of any such concern. Consequently the True Income of a group of concerns 'mainly engaged' in any type of activity will include income which accrued in other types of activity, and will *not* include all the income which actually accrued in the type of activity in question. For some of this will have accrued to multiple enterprises 'mainly engaged' in other types of productive activity. Thus the two principles laid down at the beginning of this section are infringed by the trade classification of True Income provided in this report.[1] The True Income shown for any given trade group is both increased and decreased as compared with the income actually arising from the corresponding type of activity, as a result of transfers into and out of the trade group.

Three points must be borne in mind in this connection. In the first place, what we have said means that our figures relate in fact to what the ordinary man means when he talks about 'the coal industry', 'the cotton trade' and so on. In this sense, the figures are significant even though the classification falls short of the ideal required for analytical purposes.

In the second place, many of what may be thought of as multiple concerns consist in fact of numbers of separate companies under common ownership. In these cases, each company is separately assessed, and is treated on its merits in making the trade classification. Thus the ship-building activities of a multiple concern would be separated from its steel-making activities, if the two were carried on by

[1] The same applies to that provided in the 92nd and later Annual Reports.

legally independent companies. This practice probably prevailed to a considerable extent among widely ramified multiple enterprises. Nevertheless, it will be noticed that one trade group in our tables consists explicitly of large concerns engaged in steel-making, engineering and ship-building.

In the third place, not all possible transfers of True Income between trade groups were actually realised to a significant extent. It will be seen that while some groups, like iron and steel, engineering and ship-building, overlap and are inextricably intertwined, some others, such as the professions, are virtually independent and homogeneous. In any case, some mutual cancelling out by the transfers into and out of trade groups must be expected.[1]

It cannot be assumed however that the proportionate importance of transfers of True Income resulting from the existence of multiple enterprises necessarily declines as we pass from smaller to larger aggregates of enterprises. There is in fact reason to suspect significant net transfers between major branches of activities, as well as between trade groups. In particular, such transfers have probably accrued between the manufacturing and the distributive branches. On the one hand, some income generated in the manufacture of food, in bespoke tailoring and similar activities is imputed to retail distribution; on the other hand, some income generated in distribution and transport is imputed to the manufacturing industries to which such distribution and transport were ancillary operations.

As usual when dealing with the Schedule D statistics, we have in the trade classification a set of figures which are not wholly arbitrary and chaotic, though they are certainly less precise and relevant to many economic problems than might be desired.

Because the trade groups used in the classification of True Income contain enterprises engaged in more than one kind of productive activity, the classification may not be strictly comparable with other 'trade-classifications' such as those of Gross and Net Output in the Censuses of Production. It was however intended that the trade classifications of True Income should correspond with the latter as far as possible. It will be seen that the classification of income from mining and manufacture[2] is very similar to that used in the first three Censuses of Production. As far as types of activity not covered by the Censuses

[1] Some such cancelling was apparently deliberately brought about when the 1911–12 classification was being made.
[2] Including building and public utilities.

of Production were concerned, a classification designed to retain as much information as possible was adopted and the resulting trade grouping is more or less self-explanatory. A detailed description of the contents of each trade group is given in Appendix A.

It must be remembered that during the period covered by our tables, the actual technological content of any trade group may have changed very much. Many important changes occurred in the output of industry and in the methods of producing that output. Consequently the activity carried on by any trade group in 1937 may have differed profoundly from its activity in 1910. Thus the activity of the group 'Silk and Artificial Silk' in 1937 was almost certainly very different from what it had been in 1910 because of the increased production of rayon; and equally large changes no doubt occurred in other trade groups. These effects may show themselves to some extent in changes in the relative 'size' of different trade groups. But they may not show themselves at all in the tables of True Income.[1]

An attempt has been made in the course of the discussion of the estimates arrived at to indicate cases in which these various considerations apply. For the purpose of the discussion the trade groups have been combined into seven 'major branches' of activity: extraction, manufacturing, distribution, transport, professions, miscellaneous services, and enterprises operating abroad. The composition of each of these is shown in Appendix A. All the 'major branches' of activity are built up from trade-groups, and these in turn are built up from enterprises. The classification of enterprises to form trade-groups was carried out by the Inland Revenue authorities at various times in the past. Our tabulation includes all the information contained in these original trade classifications. It is not possible to go behind it. On the other hand, our combination of the trade groups into industries and 'major branches of activity' can obviously be re-cast in many ways.

THE CLASSIFICATION OF NUMBERS OF ASSESSMENTS.

A number of considerations affect the interpretation of the trade-classifications of numbers of assessments shown in the main tables. In principle these classifications should provide information about the number of enterprises engaged in each kind of productive activity. In practice, the information they provide is not exact. Many of the considerations which affect the interpretation of the figures for True Income apply to the classification of numbers of assessments. For example, the trade classification shows, for any given trade group, only

[1] Nor in the numbers of enterprises in various trade groups.

the number of enterprises *mainly engaged* in that particular activity. Similarly, the number of assessments shown for any trade group will exclude those enterprises engaged in this activity in only a relatively minor capacity.

There are other factors which affect the number of assessments, and which must qualify any use of them as an indication of the number of enterprises operating in a year.

The number of assessments made *in* a given year may differ from the number which 'should have been' made *for* that year. This is due to the inclusion of back assessments made in respect of earlier years, and the exclusion of assessments carried forward to later years. The number of these assessments is not known, but it may be assumed to have been fairly constant from year to year, in the same way that the corresponding gross assessments were shown to be.[1] They may have accounted for a higher proportion of the total *number* of assessments than of the total *amounts* assessed. The reason for supposing this is that the back assessments included more assessments on individuals and partnerships than on companies and local authorities,[2] and the average True Income of the former was considerably less than that of the latter. This again may have implied a tendency for the back assessments to be concentrated in those trade groups such as retail distribution and the professions, where individuals and firms predominated. These considerations would not apply to the assessments made *for* any given year.

Even the number of assessments made *for* a given year was affected by the administrative practice of making more than one assessment on any given enterprise. This would happen in those cases where it was found that the original assessment had subsequently to be revised. The effect of this practice is to inflate the apparent number of enterprises assessed. Here again it is not known how many such additional assessments were made.

The numbers of assessments shown do not include the number of enterprises which made no profit, or showed a net trading loss. They do include those cases in which the whole of the trading profits are absorbed by Wear and Tear allowances, losses brought forward, and other statutory deductions.

So far, we have discussed the factors affecting the number of assessments made on a given population of enterprises. We must now mention a certain ambiguity attaching to this 'population'. We have already mentioned the inclusion of certain incomes below the exemption limit[3] in the case of non-corporate concerns. The total amount of

---

[1] See page 15 and Appendix B.   [2] 94th Report, para. 127, p. 47.   [3] Page 13.

income falling below the exemption limit and excluded from our figures was seen to be small enough to be insignificant. The same cannot be said in respect of the number of enterprises.

The number of assessments made on non-corporate concerns below the exemption limit seems to have been very large. There is evidence of this for the year 1928–29, when there were some 220,000 such assessments made, and included in the tables of this report. (The actual number was 219,155, and refers to 'original' assessments, i.e. it excludes additional assessments in respect of past years and additional assessments made later in the year in respect of omissions and undercharges). There is no reliable way of estimating the number of enterprises which were not included. The use of non-Revenue statistics, with their different coverage and timing, could not be reliably matched with the total number of *assessments* made in order to estimate the number of *enterprises* which were not assessed.

The figures for 1928–29 show the number of assessments and the amount of gross assessment, for corporate and non-corporate concerns separately, falling in the range of £1–£159. The current exemption limit was £162. In the non-corporate sector, the 219,155 assessments in this range showed a total gross assessment of £18.5 m., giving an average assessment of £85. The corresponding figures for corporate concerns are 23,226 assessments and a gross assessment of £1.3 m., giving an average assessment of £57. This difference in average assessment could be due to the exclusion of some non-corporate concerns well below the exemption limit; it could also be due to the fact that the income of an unincorporated business is often the sole livelihood of its owner, while in the case of companies the salaries of those who run the business are deducted before income is shown. A company may continue in business for some time with virtually no profit, but individuals and partnerships would not stay in business if their trading income fell below a certain level. This level will vary from case to case, and will depend partly on the level of income from other sources. The average assessment in the range below £160 varies widely from one industry to another. The figure for public utilities is £41 and that for distribution is £105. Those engaged in the former activities would presumably have wider sources of income than shopkeepers, for whom £105 would be a very low subsistence level.

Nevertheless, it is possible that a large number of small businesses were excluded because their income was below the exemption limit.

If we suppose that the true average assessment on all non-corporate concerns below the exemption limit was something less than the recorded average of £85, then a figure only slightly less than this could imply a large number of excluded businesses. For example, a true overall average of £75, obtained by including all firms and partnerships previously excluded, and postulating an average for these of £50, would imply an additional 80,000 enterprises. Other assumptions would give estimates of more or less than this number. In the example above, 80,000 represents about 8 per cent of the total number of non-corporate concerns covered by our figures.

The practical significance of this factor is that figures of average True Income per assessment cannot be taken as indicative of the average income earned by all the enterprises in any trade. Indeed, if we assume a Paretoid distribution of income, the average income depends only on the exemption limit and the Pareto index. Changes in average income from year to year would result from changes in the exemption limit or changes in the distribution of income. In other words, an overall increase in incomes would not raise the average, since there would be a compensating increase in the number of small incomes crossing the exemption limit. The 1928-29 data suggests that the distribution of incomes becomes Paretoid somewhere near to the exemption limit (i.e. the slope of the log N/log Y curve becomes constant above an income level in the range £100-£300), but the distribution might be Paretoid at a lower level if *all* incomes below the exemption limit were included in the data, and not just *some* of them. The question, therefore, as to whether there are sufficient incomes below the exemption limit to conceal any changes in the overall average level of income, remains open.

There are thus practical and theoretical objections to regarding as significant any changes which may be recorded in the average True Income of non-corporate concerns in the various trade groups over the years covered in this survey. There is nevertheless a certain interest attaching to the absolute level of the average in any year, in showing the comparative size for the various trade groups, and our main tables give this data. Even here though, differences may arise from differences between trade groups in the proportion of incomes below the exemption limit which happen to have been included. In the case of corporate concerns, where there is no exemption limit,[1] the figures of average True Income have more meaning.

---

[1] Strictly speaking there is an exemption limit at zero income, but the numbers below this level will not significantly affect the figures of average.

One further point to mention with regard to the number of assessments is that in the years covered by this report the numbers of partnerships were not separately assessed. For the year 1928–29 however the number of partners in each partnership is known; the figure for each trade group and a discussion of the data is given in Appendix E.

THE INSTITUTIONAL TYPE OF ENTERPRISES.

The main tables include analyses of the True Income and number of assessments made in each trade group according to the institutional type of enterprise assessed. The distinction made is between corporate and non-corporate enterprises. The former consist of companies, both public and private, local authorities, trade associations and similar undertakings. The non-corporate enterprises are individuals and partnerships. All the figures in this group of tables are affected by the considerations mentioned above.

For the assessment year 1911–12 figures exist of the gross assessments made on corporate and non-corporate enterprise, but there is no information as to the respective amounts of 'Other Reductions and Discharges'. It is therefore impossible to give an accurate breakdown of True Income by type of enterprise for this year. An approximate division can be arrived at by taking the same proportions as are found in the gross assessments, and this has been done for the major branches of activity analysed in Chapter III.

Figures for the individual trade groups however would be too uncertain to include in the main tables. The numbers of assessments made in 1911–12, by type of enterprise, are known precisely and these are shown in the main tables.

The division of True Income between the two types of enterprise in the later years is believed to be fairly accurate, as the trade group figure for each type of enterprise has been derived mainly from exactly known figures of gross assessment and components of 'Other Reductions and Discharges'. The True Income figures for 'All Enterprises', for the years 1927 to 1938, are in fact built up from the separate figures for corporate and non-corporate enterprises.

C

CHAPTER II

THE MAIN TOTALS

In this chapter we propose to take a brief look at the totals of the main table figures. Table 1 does in fact reproduce, for Gross True Income, the grand totals of the main tables. Before we can analyse, however, we must, for different reasons, chop two bits off the totals, and Table 1 is reproduced here for the convenience of readers who like to plot their course by arithmetical bench-marks as well as the lengthy instructions in the text.

TABLE II.1

Total True Income of concerns engaged in productive activity inside and outside the United Kingdom, gross and net of wear and tear (£m)[1]

					Gross	Net
1909	..	..	..	..	472[2]	446[2]
1927	..	..	..	..	1,014	934
1932	..	..	..	..	761	666
1936	..	..	..	..	1,096	949
1937	..	..	..	..	1,161	990
1938	..	..	..	..	1,065	886

[1] Assessed *in* 1911–12 (1909) to 1933–34 (1932); assessed *for* 1937–38 (1936) to 1939–40 (1938): excluding interest and excluding profits of agriculture.
[2] Estimated.

The first chop is one of convenience, and seemingly innocuous, namely the exclusion of 'Adventures Outside the United Kingdom' which are analysed separately in Chapter 5.[1] In fact this separation is not quite so innocuous, for reasons given more fully in that chapter. Suffice it to say here that we do not think any large error is likely if we regard what remains as being the total True Income which *arises* in the United Kingdom. For the sake of good form, however, we shall give an exact description of Table 2. The second chop is made because, for reasons given in the Appendix to Chapter 3, the figures for the Finance item in the earlier years are not comparable with those for later years. Table 2 shows Gross and Net True Income, Wear and Tear Allowances and the Number of Assessments for the groups which remain after Adventures O.U.K. and Finance have been deducted from the grand totals.

[1] The total amount of True Income from outside the United Kingdom included in the totals shown in Table 1 was, in £m:

			1909	1927	1932	1936	1937	1938
Gross	..	..	63	107	49	88	110	93
Net	..	..	59	98	36	73	94	77

TABLE II.2

True Income assessed, Wear and Tear allowances granted and Number of Assessments made: concerns operating inside the United Kingdom (excluding finance)[1]

		True Income (£m)		Wear and Tear allowances (£m)	Number of assessments (000)
		Gross	Net		
1909	..	370[2]	347[2]	23[2]	400
1927	..	840	770	70	1,029
1932	..	664	582	82	1,077
1936	..	973	842	131	1,056
1937	..	1,034	879	155	993
1938	..	965	803	162	997

[1] See note to Table 1.
[2] Estimated.

As has been explained in Chapter I, the income in Table 2 consists of that part of the True Income assessed under Schedule D which represents the *trading profits* of enterprises. The various types of *interest* assessed under Schedule D have been deducted. Small amounts of True Income (varying from £0.6 m. in 1927 to £1.5 m. in 1937) representing agricultural profits assessed under Schedule D have also been deducted. Before 1933 the trading surpluses of co-operative societies were not assessed to income tax, consequently the figures in Table 2 for 1909 and 1927 exclude them altogether. In 1933 legislation was introduced rendering such surpluses liable to standard rate of income tax, but excluding 'divi'. Thus for the assessment year 1933–4 onwards the figures in Table 2 include the amount of retained profits *plus* share and loan interest of co-operative societies.[1]

Although profits below the exemption limit are not assessed to income tax, a (small) part of them is included in the figures.[2] With

[1] The amounts of 'Trading Surplus *minus* Dividends' for co-operative societies, in the calendar years approximately corresponding to the rows of Table 2, as obtained from the Registry of Friendly Societies Statistical Summary of Co-operative Societies are as follows:

	1932 (1933–4)	1936 (1937–8)	1937 (1938–9)	1938 (1939–40)
			(£ million)	
Retail Societies	6.3	6.6	6.7	7.3
Wholesale and Productive Societies	2.0	2.2	2.1	2.7

It may be of interest to record here the whole trading surplus of co-operative societies for 1927, and the 'divi' for the years after the tax change. These are the 'profits' of co-operatives which have not been included in the figures in Tables 2.

	1927 (1928–9)	1932 (1933–4)	1936 (1937–8)	1937 (1938–9)	1938 (1939–40)
			(£ million)		
Retail Societies	23.2	18.6	21.8	23.0	23.6
Wholesale and Productive Societies	3.1	1.9	3.0	3.2	3.3

The above breakdown is not available for 1909.

[2] See Chapter I, p. 13, for an explanation of how this occurs.

these exceptions, Table 2 shows the total True Income (other than interest) assessed, the Wear and Tear Allowances granted and the number of assessments made on concerns operating mainly inside the United Kingdom in the six years for which we have made trade classifications, excluding Finance and Agriculture. These figures refer, in effect, to productive activity carried on geographically inside the United Kingdom. Strictly speaking, they refer to British concerns whose principal fixed assets were in the United Kingdom. This is taken to include concerns such as British shipping companies and export-import concerns whose main offices were in the United Kingdom. The concerns excluded are, typically, British-owned railway companies, mines and plantations in other countries, besides, of course, the Finance item inside the United Kingdom and the small amount of Agricultural profits under Schedule D.

The qualifications that must be borne in mind in interpreting the figures shown in Table 2 have been discussed in Chapter I. These considerations apart, the following broad conclusions can be drawn from the figures.

In the first place, the gross trading profits as defined for income tax purposes accruing from productive activity in the United Kingdom (excluding Finance and Agriculture) amounted to about £1,000 million in each of the last three years of the inter-war period. This part of the productive sector of the British economy consisted at that time of about one million concerns. Sums allowed by the authorities to meet wear and tear amounted to about £150 million, apart from those sums allowed by way of repairs and renewals. In similar round terms, we can say that in the three years about 1909, the gross trading profits of concerns operating inside the United Kingdom amounted to rather less than £400 million and the number of concerns to about 400,000. Sums allowed for wear and tear in these years amounted to about £20 million in addition to the allowances made on the repairs and renewals basis. The calendar time reference of the first row of Table 2 is 'about 1909'. Let us take each of these figures as 100. We average the figures of the last three rows and give a time reference of 'the late nineteen-thirties'. We thus obtain rough index figures for the change in the various items over a time span of just under thirty years as follows:

Gross True Income	... ...	270
Net True Income ...	... ...	240
Wear and Tear allowances ...	...	650
Number of assessments	... ...	250

The disproportionate increase in Wear and Tear allowances is partly the result of changes in administrative practice described in Chapter I (pp. 11, 12).

As indications of a trend these figures are about as shaky as they can be. We have only one set of assessments for the pre-1914–18 war benchmark, and as we shall see in a moment there were considerable intervening fluctuations in the various figures.

Most of the increase in True Income, Wear and Tear allowances and number of assessments occurred before the assessment year 1927. The number of assessments shows a rise to the early 'thirties and a slow fall thereafter. But, as has been pointed out, the number of assessments made in (or for) any given assessment year is more sensitive than the amount of True Income to changes in the effective exemption limits. The reduction of this limit in 1931 may well explain the apparent peak figure for 1932 in Table 2, so that it seems impossible to draw any definite inferences from the variations in the number of assessments.

It will be seen from the last five rows in Table 2 that the fluctuations of True Income are in accordance with other indicators of the general pattern of economic activity in this period, but the identification of profits with calendar years is uncertain and the 'cyclical' pattern of True Income shown here should be treated with caution.

In Table 3, the total True Income assessed and number of assessments made on concerns operating inside the United Kingdom (excluding Finance and Agriculture) are divided between corporate and non-corporate concerns. The corporate concerns consisted of companies (both public and private), local authorities, trading associations and similar concerns. Non-corporate concerns consisted of individual traders and unincorporated partnerships.

TABLE II.3

Gross True Income assessed and number of assessments made on corporate and non-corporate concerns operating in the United Kingdom.[1]

| | | Gross True Income (£m) | | Number of Assessments (000) | |
		Corporate	Non-corporate	Corporate	Non-corporate
1909	..	N.A.	N.A.	42	358
1927	..	460	379	83	946
1932	..	365	298	84	992
1936	..	621	352	99	957
1937	..	694	340	104	889
1938	..	648	317	102	875

[1] See note to Table 1.

It will be seen that while the *number* of non-corporate concerns, to judge from the number of assessments made on them, was between 8 and 12 times as great as the number of corporate concerns, the corporate concerns received a larger share of *Gross True Income* than the non-corporate concerns. The share of corporate concerns in total Gross True Income in the five years for which it can be estimated was (as a percentage of the total):

1927 ...	...	55
1932 ...	...	55
1936 ...	...	64
1937 ...	...	67
1938 ...	...	67

The division of Gross True Income for 1909 is not known, but some indication of the sizes of the two shares is provided by the division of the Gross Assessment in 1911–12 (1909) (i.e. before making the relevant deductions). The share of corporate enterprise was 59 per cent. The figures available, therefore, suggest that the share of corporate enterprise in Gross True Income declined slightly between about 1909 and the end of the 1920's, and increased considerably in the second half of the 1930's. The apparent decline between the assessment years 1911–12 (1909) and 1928–29 (1927) may be partly due to the fact that the figures for these years are not strictly comparable. But some decline might be expected as a result of the growth, which may be assumed, of trades and industries like distribution and road transport in which non-corporate enterprise was predominant. The lowering of the effective exemption limit between 1909 and 1927 would tend to increase the proportion of True Income assessed on very small enterprises, most of which would presumably be non-corporate concerns. The increase in the share of corporate enterprise after 1932 must be supposed to reflect both a tendency towards the incorporation of non-corporate enterprises, and a relative increase in the average size of the corporate ones compared with non-corporate ones.

For reasons already explained,[1] figures of average Gross True Income per assessment cannot be used to measure the change in size of non-corporate concerns over time. The figures of average Gross True Income of *corporate* concerns do however provide evidence of their increasing size over the period 1927 to 1938. This tendency was clear in spite of a very marked decline in the average Gross True Income

[1] Ch. I, pp. 23, 24.

between 1927 and 1932. The following figures show that the overall
increase between the two good years 1927 and 1937 was of the order of
20 per cent.

Average Gross True Income of corporate enterprise:

     1927: £5,570
     1932: £4,350
     1936: £6,250
     1937: £6,700
     1938: £6,340

CHAPTER III

PROFITS OF SIX MAJOR BRANCHES OF ACTIVITY

The concerns operating inside the United Kingdom have been classified in six major groups, corresponding as closely as possible to six major branches of productive activity. These are extractive industry, manufacturing, distribution, transport, the professions and miscellaneous services. The contents of each group are defined in Appendix A, and are shown in the main tables. Roughly speaking, the 'extractive' group consists of concerns mainly engaged in mining and quarrying; the 'manufacturing' group consists of all enterprises mainly engaged in the physical transformation of materials, and includes building and contracting as well as gas, water and electricity undertakings. The 'extractive' and 'manufacturing' groups together therefore correspond roughly with the industries covered by the Censuses of Production. The distributive group consists of all concerns whose *main* activity was distributing merchandise: in addition to wholesale merchants and retail shopkeepers it includes hotels and restaurants. The transport group includes merchant shipping and the operation of docks, harbours and canals, as well as inland transport by rail and road. The professional group includes all members of the various professions shown in the main tables who were 'trading' on their own account: it does not include professional persons, such as doctors, teachers or engineers employed by other enterprises, local authorities or the central government. The 'miscellaneous services' group includes concerns such as public amusements, crematoria and lodging houses.

As has been explained in Chapter I, the division of True Income among these major groups of concerns does not correspond exactly with a hypothetical division of trading profits according to the productive activities from which they accrued. Some concerns in the extractive group were also engaged in subsidiary manufacturing activities, while much mining and quarrying were carried on by concerns allocated to the manufacturing group. Similarly, many manufacturing concerns using their own road vehicles, or owning their own retail establishments were engaged in both transport and distribution. On the other hand, the concerns here classified as 'distributive' included many which also manufactured some of the goods they distributed.

These included both large and small food manufacturing concerns, and concerns, generally small, such as bespoke tailors. Such concerns, if engaged *mainly* in distribution, are included in the trade-group 'Retail, semi-industrial', to distinguish them from the purely retailing concerns classified as 'Retail, distributive'. We have already pointed out that the professional group covers only a part of the activities of professional persons.

The net effects of this lack of perfect correspondence between the actual activities of concerns within a particular group, and the type of activity represented by the title of that group are probably not very important in practice. At the same time, the figures based on this six-fold classification and presented in this chapter cannot be accepted at their face-value and compared, without further analysis, with figures from other sources which appear to relate to the same industry group. Finally, we are concerned in this chapter only with concerns operating mainly in the United Kingdom.

(i) Gross True Income.

Table 1[1] shows the Gross True Income of the six major industry groups. In Table 2 the figures are expressed as a percentage of the total Gross True Income in each year. It will be seen that the six groups were of very unequal importance as sources of profit.

Looking first at the figures in Table 1, we can see that the main increases during the period 1909 to 1927 occurred in manufacturing and distribution, with Gross True Income in the latter year of £325 m. and £310 m. respectively. In 1932 each of these activities recorded a Gross True Income 23.4 per cent down on 1927, reflecting a remarkable similarity in the effect on their respective fortunes of the Depression. The later 1930's, however, produced conditions more favourable to manufacturing enterprise than to the distributive trades. The annual average Gross True Income during the last three years was £439 m. in manufacturing as opposed to £300 m. in distribution. This divergence reflects the increasing importance of rearmament and investment expenditure prior to World War II, as in shown by the figures for gross true income in engineering and building activities during this period.

Elsewhere in the economy, the increases in Gross True Income during the thirty year span of these figures were very uneven. Taking an average for the last three years, the changes since 1909 were: from £19 m. to £28 m. in extraction, from £73 m. to £105 m. in transport,

[1] The tables referred to in this chapter are grouped together at the end of the chapter.

from £31 m. to £88 m. in the professions and from £7 m. to £32 m. in the miscellaneous trades. In 1927 extraction was the only major group with a lower gross true income than in 1909; and in 1932, the miscellaneous group was the only one with a higher gross true income than in 1927.

The changes in relative importance during the six years covered in this survey are shown by the percentage distributions in Table 2.

The proportion of total gross true income accruing to undertakings in the manufacturing, distributive and transport groups was around 85 per cent throughout the six years. During this period, however, the individual shares of these three groups changed considerably. The greatest change was in the share attributable to transport, which was 20 per cent in 1909, and then remained at 10 or 11 per cent throughout the inter-war period. While the transport share fell, the share of distribution increased, from 27 per cent in 1909 to 37 per cent in 1927. The shares of manufacturing and distribution were more or less equal in 1927 and 1932, having both declined very slightly in the latter year. In the final three years, 1936 to 1938, manufacturing increased its share to over 44 per cent, and distribution took second place at around 30 per cent. We have already commented on this divergence between these two main groups.

The share of the professional group remained very constant at about 9 per cent, except for the year 1932 when it rose to 10.5 per cent. The earnings of this group did fall during the Depression, but not by so much as profits generally. The figures suggest that professional earnings follow an upward trend in profits very closely, but are more rigid downwards.

For the other two groups, Table 2 shows a decline in the importance of extraction since before the First War, and a continuing increase in the share earned by the miscellaneous group throughout the inter-war period.

The figures for the three main groups may not be wholly in accordance with expectations. It might have been expected that the shares of the distributive and transport groups would have increased, in view of the generally supposed tendency of the distributive sector of the economy to grow faster than the manufacturing sector in the inter-war period. The full significance of the figures concerning these three groups in Tables 1 and 2 cannot be understood, however, until they have been analysed in greater detail. To some extent, they probably reflect changes in the structure of the economy, as a result of which 'distributive' and 'transport' activities came to be carried on to an increasing extent by 'manufacturing' concerns, a tendency made possible by the development of road transport. Also, to the extent that government contracts are responsible for the increase in the manufacturing share during the immediate pre-war period, the shares recorded for the distributive sector in these years will understate its relative importance in those fields of activity where it had a function.

By way of summary, Table 3 compares the marginal rates of increase of the six main groups from 1909 to the late 1930's. (Figures for the three years 1936 to 1938 are averaged). Total Gross True Income increased by £621 million in just under thirty years. Nearly half this increase occurred in manufacturing, and about a third occurred in distribution.

(ii) NET TRUE INCOME.

The Net True Income assessed on concerns in the six major industry groups is shown in Table 4. The main difference between the pattern of the figures in this table and that of the Gross True Income figures in Table I is that the Net True Income of the distributive group was greater than that of the manufacturing group in 1927 and 1932. One can see also that in the other four years the difference between the True Income of these two groups is considerably narrowed after the deduction of the Wear and Tear allowances. Another change in the pattern is in the relative amounts of True Income earned by the transport and professional groups. The gross figures show transport with a higher True Income in each of the inter-war years except 1932, whereas the net figures indicate a higher True Income accruing to the professions in each of these five years.

Table 5, showing the percentage distribution of total Net True Income, brings out this change in the relative importance of the transport and professional groups. The proportions were about 8 per cent and 10 per cent respectively. The table also shows the manufacturing group earning a rather smaller share of total net profits than of gross profits, and the distributive group earning a rather larger share of net than of gross profits. Otherwise the general pattern is very similar to that shown in Table 2: again, the manufacturing, distributive and transport groups earned about 85 per cent of the total Net True Income in each of the six years.

The Wear and Tear allowances granted to concerns in the six major groups are given in Table 6. As has already been explained, the economic significance of these figures is limited by the changes which were made from time to time in the statutory provisions for depreciation. But although one cannot deduce the trend in the actual amounts of capital consumption in any one group, one can see in general outline the relative incidence of these costs among the six groups in any one year.

Table 6 shows that in all six years the greater part of the allowances was granted to the manufacturing and transport groups. Together, these two groups accounted for about 90 per cent of the total in 1909 and around 80 per cent in the five inter-war years. It must be remembered that the depreciation of the plant and machinery of railway companies (included in the transport group) was mainly dealt with on the 'repairs and renewals' basis. Allowances made in this way are deducted before the assessment of Gross True Income, and are not shown in any of our statistics. This must have an appreciable effect on the comparability of the Wear and Tear figures for railways and the transport group as a whole. In Chapter I,[1] it was seen that the written-down value of railway rolling stock on which the repairs and renewals method was used was estimated at £132 m. for 1930.

The only other group with a significant share of the allowances was distribution. This group accounted for under 5 per cent of the total in 1909, but its share was around 15 per cent in the inter-war years. These three groups therefore absorbed about 95 per cent of the allowances in each of the six years, while earning about 85 per cent of the total True Income.

To get an idea of the proportion of gross income which had to be set off against depreciation, Table 7 has been set out showing the Wear and Tear allowances of the six major groups as a percentage of Gross True Income. One can see the general tendency of the allowances to absorb a higher proportion of gross income throughout the period. This is of course partly due to increases in the statutory rates of allowance. It must also be partly due to a more extensive use of capital equipment, especially in the manufacturing, transport and extractive industries. Whatever the relative importance of these two factors, the allowances in 1938 took twice the proportion of Gross True Income as in 1927.

The highest proportion occurred in transport, rising from 26 per cent in 1927 to 36 per cent in 1937. The rise to 46 per cent in 1938 is partly due to the extra £10 m. granted to railways, which were changing in this year from the renewals to the Wear and Tear method. An increase in the proportion of True Income set off against Wear and Tear

[1] Page 11.

could anyway be expected from the changing structure of the transport group. Apart from railways, the main trade groups were shipping and road transport. Ships have a long life, and therefore carry a low annual rate of Wear and Tear (3 to 5 per cent); road vehicles were assumed to be written off over four or five years and the rates were therefore 20 to 25 per cent. The ratio of Wear and Tear to profit is given by $1/L.r$, where L is the life of capital and r the rate of return on capital. With the increasing importance of road transport relative to shipping during the inter-war period, the average value of L for transport as a whole would fall, giving a higher proportion of Wear and Tear to be met from Gross True Income. The rate of return in road transport would have to be several times greater than in shipping in order to offset the effect of decreasing capital life. It is perhaps unexpected to find that the Wear and Tear allowances took a higher proportion of Gross True Income in Extraction than in manufacturing during most of the inter-war period, and this is despite a higher rate of growth in profits in the extractive industry. From 1927 to 1937 the proportions in extractive and manufacturing industries increased from 12 per cent to 21 per cent and from 11 per cent to 18 per cent respectively.

(iii) NUMBER OF ASSESSMENTS.

Table 8 shows the number of assessments made on concerns in each of the six major groups. The number of assessment in the extractive group declined steadily from nearly 6,000 in 1909 to about 3,400 in 1938. This decline may indicate a decline in the number of autonomous concerns mainly engaged in mining and quarrying. It is unlikely to be due mainly to purely administrative factors, such as the exclusion from our figures of concerns making net losses. The number of cases would probably be smaller in the assessments made for 1937 than in any other assessment year. It must therefore be interpreted as reflecting the winding-up of some concerns, the amalgamation of others within the extractive group, and the incorporation of others in concerns mainly engaged in other types of activity.

The number of assessments in the manufacturing group also declined during the inter-war period. The number in 1927 (106,000) was considerably greater than the number in 1909 (63,000), as a result mainly of the real expansion of this kind of productive activity. During the inter-war period, however, the number of assessments tended to decline. Only 93,000 assessments were made on this group for 1937 and only 90,000 in 1938. On the whole, this decline may be taken to reflect a consolidation of the ownership of enterprise in this part of the economy. It will be seen from Table 8 that the changes in the number of assessments in the manufacturing group between the years covered by our figures are not great enough to account for the changes in the total number of assessments between those years.

The distributive group was by far the most numerous of the six major groups. The number of assessments recorded for 1909 is 207,000 and for 1927 it is 679,000.[1] How far this numerical difference represents a real increase in the numbers engaged in distribution is not easy to say. The general price level rose by about a half between these two years, while the nominal exemption limit remained about the same; in other words the real exemption limit fell by about a third. We would therefore expect a certain number of non-corporate concerns, unrecorded in 1909, to have reached a level of money income by 1927 high enough for an assessment to be made. The number of assessments on non-corporate concerns increased from 197,000 to 653,000; it is unlikely that more than a relatively small proportion of this 456,000 increase represented concerns which existed but were unrecorded in 1909. A certain number of concerns below the exemption limit in 1909 would anyway be included in the total number of assessments. Furthermore, even if a large number of concerns crossed the line between 1909 and 1927, making the recorded increase apparent rather than real, a real increase could still occur through an increase in the number of unrecorded concerns below the limit. The matter cannot be resolved precisely, but some indication may be obtained from the increase in the number of assessments made on corporate concerns, where there is no exemption limit. These increased from under 10,000 in 1909 to over 25,000 in 1927. A similar rate of increase in the non-corporate sector would account for about two-thirds of the recorded increase of 456,000.

The number of assessments on the distributive group also increased between 1927 and 1932, when it reached 719,000. This increase of about 40,000 during the period of the Depression may seem remarkable, but it cannot be assumed that it was due to an increase in the number of distributive concerns. The Autumn Budget of 1931, by lowering the

---

[1] There are no official figures for the number of distributive concerns in these years. The Censuses of Population in 1921 and 1931 give the number of proprietors and managers (male and female) of wholesale and retail businesses in Great Britain. These numbers compare with the number of assessments on wholesale and retail concerns as follows:

Proprietors and Managers (G.B.)			*No. of assessments* (U.K.)		
1921	..	600,000	1927	..	600,000
1931	..	712,000	1932	..	642,000

The figures suggest a real increase in the number of distributive concerns.

exemption limit, brought in large numbers of small traders previously excluded from our figures. In fact this Budget increased the total number of incomes over the exemption limit by two-thirds, and if we assume that small traders had an income distribution similar to that for all personal incomes over the range around this level, then it seems possible that the total number of small traders actually declined at this time. The figures for later years do show a decline in the number of assessments on this group; they fell to 652,000 in 1938.

The number of assessments on the transport group increased from about 9,000 in 1909 to about 33,000 in 1927. This was mainly the result of the development of road transport between 1910 and the 1920's. The number of assessments on this group increased during the inter-war period, amounting to nearly 38,000 in 1936.

The number of assessments on the professional group rose from 75,000 in 1909 to about 107,000 in 1927, and to 115,000 in 1936, declining to about 109,000 in 1938. Although, as is shown later, most of these assessments were made on 'individuals and partnerships', and not on companies, these figures are an imperfect indication of the number of professional *persons* practising on their own account in the years in question. For in all the years of our series partnerships were assessed as single units without regard to the number of partners in each. The numbers of members of partnerships assessed in 1927 is known and the figures are given in Appendix E.

Table 9 shows the percentage distribution of the total number of assessments among the six major groups. The table shows the numerical preponderance of assessments made on the distributive group. Even before the First World War, one half of the total number of Schedule D assessments on trading profits were made on concerns mainly engaged in distribution. During the inter-war period, two-thirds of the total number of assessments were made on such concerns. Concerns mainly engaged in manufacturing accounted for only 16 per cent of the total number of assessments made in 1909 and only 9 per cent in the inter-war period. Similarly, assessments on the professional group made up 19 per cent of the total number in 1909 and 11 per cent in the inter-war period.

(iv) AVERAGE G.T.I. PER ASSESSMENT.[1]

Table 10 shows the average Gross True Income per assessment in the six major industrial groups. Broadly speaking, these six groups fall

[1] The reader is referred to Chapter I pp. 23, 24, for a discussion of the reliability of estimates of average profit.

into one of two classes: those like extraction, manufacturing and transport with an average of over £2,000, and those like distribution, professions and miscellaneous services with an average of under £1,000. It will be seen in Table 12 that this dichotomy corresponds broadly with that between industries with a high or a low proportion of Gross True Income assessed against corporate enterprises.

In 1909, the average assessment was much greater in the transport group than in any other. The relatively great importance of the railway companies before the First War explains the high figure of £8,350 for transport in 1909. After the war the average dropped considerably, due to the appearance of a large number of small operators in road transport. The average was under £3,000 in all the inter-war years except 1937.

The average in manufacturing was just over £2,000 in 1909, and our figures show no appreciable rise in this level until the end of the 1930's when it reached £5,000. In extraction, the average was in all years higher than in manufacturing, but, as in the latter case, there was a considerable increase in the late 1930's. It rose from £3,500 in 1932 to £8,500 in 1938. We have already noted an increase in total Gross True Income and a decrease in number of assessments on this group during this period.

In the distributive group the average in the inter-war period (£450) was about the same as in 1909, in spite of the considerable rise in the general price level. In 1932 the average was 30 per cent lower in current money terms than it had been over twenty years before, but this may be largely due to the fall in the exemption limit.

The average in the professional group was about £400 in 1909 and rose to £800 at the end of the inter-war period. As has been pointed out, already, the average assessment in this group does not represent exactly the average income from professional activity of the members of the various professions. Partnerships were assessed as units, so that the figures in Table 10 *overstate* the average income per person.

(v) CORPORATE AND NON-CORPORATE ENTERPRISE.

Section (i) of this chapter outlines the growth in Gross True Income of the major industrial groups. A breakdown of these figures into the profits of the corporate and non-corporate sectors shows that while the former was expanding during the inter-war period, the latter was in most cases contracting. The separate figures are shown in Table 11.

Comparing the two relatively prosperous years 1927 and 1937, corporate income increased 50 per cent, from £460 m. to over £690 m., while non-corporate income fell by 10 per cent, from £380 m. to £340 m.

The principal changes in the Gross True Income of the non-corporate sector occurred in manufacturing and distribution. In the ten years, these two fell by £15 m. and £40 m. respectively. At the same time, the Gross True Income of the corporate sector increased in manufacturing by £150 m., and in distribution by £40 m. In transport there was a small increase in non-corporate income of nearly £3 m., while corporate income rose by over £20 m. Only in the professions was there evidence of a strong upward trend, but in this case only a very small number of practices were incorporated.

In manufacturing the fall in non-corporate Gross True Income was matched by a corresponding fall in the number of assessments. The average profit, in other words, probably did not change much. In distribution, on the other hand, the number of assessments on non-corporate concerns did not fall as much as their Gross True Income, but in this sector the number of assessments is a particularly poor guide to the number of enterprises operating.

The changing relative importance of the corporate sector is brought out in Table 12 which shows, for each of four years, the proportion of Gross True Income which was earned by the corporate sector, and the corresponding proportion of numbers. For the sake of comparison, figures are given for 1909 based on the gross *assessments* made in that year (i.e. before the various deductions which yield the G.T.I. figure). If these figures can be taken as more or less comparable they suggest a relative strengthening of the *non-corporate* sector over the period 1909 to 1927, mainly in the transport group.[1] In extraction and manufacturing it was the corporate sector which advanced in this period, both numerically and in relative profits. This trend continued throughout the inter-war period, until in both cases over 90 per cent of the profits in these two groups were earned by the 50 per cent or so of businesses which were incorporated.

In distribution it is particularly difficult to plot the changes in the number of non-corporate concerns, but the number of corporate concerns appears to have increased substantially, in line with a large increase in True Income. Over the inter-war period it is clear that in distribution the corporate sector was gaining in importance.

---

[1] They may of course not be comparable; there may have been a larger number of concerns excluded below the exemption limit in 1909 than in 1927. Since the real exemption limit was lower in 1927 than in 1909 this is possible, but one cannot tell to what extent this factor would account for the apparent increase in non-corporate numbers and profits.

D

The year 1909 finds transport dominated by the large companies in shipping and railways. The corporate sector accounted for about 95 per cent of the profits in this group, and constituted only a third of the total numbers. The entry of large numbers of small road operators after the First War, together with the decline in railway profits, made this industry less top-heavy. By 1932 only 11 per cent of enterprises were corporate and their share of the total Gross True Income was 84 per cent. However, five years later both these proportions had increased.

The overall picture is one of great diversity between the groups as to the relative importance of the corporate sector, with the 'productive' trades becoming more organised on a corporate basis, and the 'service' trades, on balance, first expanding in the non-corporate sphere and then the opposite process taking place.

The average Gross True Income in the corporate and non-corporate sectors is shown in Table 13. The three years for which figures are shown, 1927, 1932 and 1937, correspond very roughly with boom-slump-boom years of the trade-cycle. As measures of average profit per enterprise the figures should be regarded only as orders of magnitude.

Looking first at corporate enterprise, the main difference between these figures and those in Table 10 (which give averages for *all* enterprises) is the very high figure for transport compared with any other industrial group. This does not of course imply greater profitability in transport than, say, manufacturing. The reverse was the case, especially in 1937, when the average for transport was nearly £18,000 as opposed to £10,000 in manufacturing. Again, in transport the average was lower in 1937 than in 1927, while in manufacturing the average increased by about £2,300.

The increase in the overall average, from £5,550 to £6,700, was mainly due to the growth of the manufacturing group. In distribution, the only other numerically large group, the average Gross True Income barely rose at all. Manufacturing was in fact the only group in which there was an appreciable increase both in numbers of assessments and in the average Gross True Income per assessment. The number of assessments on corporate and non-corporate concerns are shown separately in Table 14. In manufacturing the number of assessments on corporate concerns rose from 35,000 to 42,000 in the period 1927 to 1937; in distribution the increase was from 26,000 to 37,000. Together, they accounted for three-quarters of all assessments made on corporate concerns.

In the non-corporate sector the average income was very much lower than for corporate enterprise, and would be shown as lower still if all the excluded businesses below the exemption limit were included. The professions, with an average of £800 in 1937, show the highest figure. Miscellaneous services, with £150, show the lowest in all three years. In 1927 this average was itself below the current exemption limit, which suggests that many such services were performed by persons with other sources of income. No significance can be given to annual changes in these averages, but the conclusion of this section must be that, during the inter-war period, the firms and partnerships played an increasingly minor role in the economic progress which occurred.

The Tables for Chapter III

The following tables refer to six major industrial groups, comprising between them all enterprises operating mainly in the U.K., but excluding assessments on Agriculture, Finance and investment income. For a discussion of the reliability of the various statistics, see 'Statistical Notes to the Main Tables'.

Contents

TABLE III.1
Gross True Income of concerns in six major industrial Groups.[1]
£ million

		1909	1927	1932	1936	1937	1938
Extraction	..	19	17	15	27	29	29
Manufacturing	..	139	325	249	425	459	433
Distribution	..	100	310	237	310	309	280
Transport	..	73	90	65	94	116	105
Professions	..	31	75	70	89	89	85
Misc. services	..	7	25	28	29	32	34
Total ..	..	370	840	664	973	1,034	965

[1]Assessed *in* 1911–12 to 1933–34; assessed *for* 1937–38 to 1939–40.

TABLE III.2
Percentage distribution of Gross True Income among six major industrial groups.[1]

		1909	1927	1932	1936	1937	1938
Extraction	..	5	2	2	3	3	3
Manufacturing	..	38	39	37	44	44	45
Distribuion	..	27	37	36	32	30	29
Transport	..	20	11	10	10	11	11
Professions	..	8	9	11	9	9	9
Misc. services	..	2	3	4	3	3	4

[1] See footnote to Table 1.

TABLE III.3
Increase in Gross True Income between 1909 and 1936–38 (average)

			Increase £m.	Per cent distribution of the increase	Per cent distribution of the 1909 total
Extraction	..	..	+ 9	1.4	5.2
Manufacturing	..	..	+300	48.3	37.6
Distribution	..	..	+200	32.2	27.0
Transport	..	..	+ 32	5.1	19.8
Professions	..	..	+ 57	9.2	8.3
Misc. services	..	..	+ 24	3.9	2.0
Total	..	..	+621	100.0	100.0

TABLE III.4
Net True Income of six major industrial groups.[1]   £ million

		1909	1927	1932	1936	1937	1938
Extraction	..	19	15	11	21	23	23
Manufacturing	..	129	290	206	355	379	349
Distribution	..	99	301	225	290	287	260
Transport	..	63	67	44	62	74	57
Professions	..	31	74	69	88	88	83
Misc. services	..	7	23	26	27	29	31
Total ..	..	347	770	582	842	879	803

[1] See footnote to Table 1.

TABLE III.5
Percentage distribution of Net True Income among six major industrial groups.[1]

		1909	1927	1932	1936	1937	1938
Extraction	..	5	2	2	3	3	3
Manufacturing	..	37	38	35	42	43	43
Distribution	..	28	39	39	34	33	32
Transport	..	18	9	8	7	8	7
Professions	..	9	10	12	10	10	10
Misc. services	..	2	3	5	3	3	4

[1] See footnote to Table 1.

TABLE III.6
Wear and Tear allowances against Gross True Income of six major industrial groups.[1]   £ million

		1909	1927	1932	1936	1937	1938
Extraction	..	0.9	2.0	4.2	5.4	6.0	5.4
Manufacturing	..	10.5	34.2	42.5	69.2	80.6	84.2
Distribution	..	1.0	8.9	12.1	20.5	21.1	20.3
Transport	..	9.8	23.3	20.8	31.9	42.2	48.0
Professions	..	—	0.5	0.8	1.3	1.4	1.5
Misc. services	..	0.5	1.3	1.5	2.6	3.1	2.9
Total ..	..	22.7	70.2	81.9	130.8	154.5	162.4

[1] See footnote to Table 1.

TABLE III.7
Wear and Tear allowances as percentage of Gross True Income of six major industrial groups.[1]

		1909	1927	1932	1936	1937	1938
Extraction	..	5	12	27	20	21	19
Manufacturing	..	8	11	17	16	18	19
Distribution	..	1	3	5	7	7	7
Transport	..	13	26	32	34	36	46
Professions	..	—	1	1	1	2	2
Misc. services	..	7	5	5	9	10	9
All groups	..	6	8	12	13	15	17

[1] See footnote to Table 1.

TABLE III.8
Number of Assessments in six major industrial groups.[1]   *Thousands*

		1909	1927	1932	1936	1937	1938
Extraction	..	5.9	5.0	4.4	3.6	3.6	3.4
Manufacturing	..	63	106	98	99	93	90
Distribution	..	207	679	719	706	667	652
Transport	..	9	33	37	38	32	36
Professions	..	75	107	115	115	110	109
Misc. services	..	39	99	104	94	87	87
Total ..	..	400	1,029	1,077	1,056	993	977

[1] See footnote to Table 1.

TABLE III.9
Percentage distribution of Number of Assessments among six major industrial groups[1]

		1909	1927	1932	1936	1937	1938
Extraction	..	1.5	0.5	0.4	0.3	0.4	0.3
Manufacturing	..	16	10	9	9	9	9
Distribution	..	52	66	67	67	67	67
Transport	..	2	3	3	4	3	4
Professions	..	19	10	11	11	11	11
Misc. services	..	10	10	10	9	9	9

[1] See footnote to Table 1.

TABLE III.10
Average Gross True Income per assessment on concerns in six major industrial groups[1] £[2]

		1909	1927	1932	1936	1937	1938
Extraction	..	3,300	3,350	3,550	7,400	8,100	8,450
Manufacturing	..	2,200	3,050	2,550	4,250	4,950	4,800
Distribution	..	500	450	350	450	450	450
Transport	..	8,350	2,700	1,750	2,450	3,600	2,850
Professions	..	400	700	600	750	800	800
Misc. services	..	200	250	250	300	350	400
All concerns	..	900	800	600	900	1,050	1,000

[1] See footnote to Table 1.
[2] Figures are rounded to the nearest £50.

TABLE III.11
Gross True Income of corporate (C) and non-corporate (N.C.) concerns in six major industrial groups.[1] £ million

		1927		1932		1936		1937		1938	
		C.	N.C.	C.	N.C.	C.	N.C.	C.	N.C.	C.	N.C.
Extraction	..	15	2	14	1	25	2	28	1	28	1
Manufacturing	..	272	53	216	32	384	41	421	38	401	32
Distribution	..	82	228	63	174	115	195	122	187	104	176
Transport	..	78	12	54	11	79	15	101	14	91	14
Professions	..	1	73	1	69	2	87	2	87	2	83
Misc. services	..	12	12	16	11	17	12	20	12	23	11
Total	..	460	379	365	298	621	352	694	340	648	317

[1] See footnote to Table 1.

TABLE III.12

Gross True Income and Number of Assessments of corporate enterprises as a percentage of the total in each of the six major industrial groups[1]

	1909 G.T.I.[2]	1909 No.	1927 G.T.I.	1927 No.	1932 G.T.I.	1932 No.	1937 G.T.I.	1937 No.
Extraction ..	85	27	89	41	92	44	96	53
Manufacturing ..	76	31	84	33	87	35	92	45
Distribution ..	25	5	26	4	26	4	39	6
Transport ..	95	33	87	13	84	11	88	18
Professions ..	2	1	2	1	1	1	2	1
Misc. services ..	52	19	50	15	59	14	63	17
All groups ..	59	10	55	8	55	8	67	10

[1] See footnote to Table 1.
[2] Percentage of gross *assessments* made in 1909.

TABLE III.13

Average Gross True Income per assessment on corporate and non-corporate concerns in six major industrial groups.[1] £[2]

	Corporate 1927	Corporate 1932	Corporate 1937	Non-corporate 1927	Non-corporate 1932	Non-corporate 1937
Extraction ..	7,200	7,400	14,550	650	500	750
Manufacturing ..	7,700	6,350	10,000	750	500	750
Distribution ..	3,200	2,250	3,250	350	250	300
Transport ..	18,800	13,050	17,850	400	350	550
Professions ..	1,050	750	1,300	700	600	800
Misc. services ..	850	1,150	1,350	150	150	150
All groups ..	5,550	4,350	6,700	400	300	400

[1] See footnote to Table 1.
[2] Figures are rounded to the nearest £50.

TABLE III.14

Number of Assessments on corporate and non-corporate concerns in six major industrial groups.[1] *Thousands*

	Corporate 1927	Corporate 1932	Corporate 1937	Non-corporate 1927	Non-corporate 1932	Non-corporate 1937
Extraction ..	2.1	1.9	1.9	2.9	2.4	1.7
Manufacturing ..	35	34	42	71	64	51
Distribution ..	26	28	37	653	691	629
Transport ..	4.2	4.1	5.7	29	33	27
Professions ..	1.2	1.3	1.6	106	114	108
Misc. services ..	14	14	15	84	89	72
Total ..	83	84	104	946	992	889

[1] See footnote to Table 1.

APPENDIX TO CHAPTER III

The concerns classified in the Finance group have been excluded from the discussion in the main body of this report. They are also excluded from the U.K. Totals in the Main Tables, being shown separately at the end. The reason for this exclusion is that the Gross True Income figures shown here refer to *trading* profits only, income from interest being excluded from all trade groups. Since income from interest constitutes a major portion of the total *commercial* profits of many financial enterprises, a comparison between the trading profits in finance and in other activities would give a very misleading picture. Furthermore, the difference between trading profits and commercial profits in the finance sector appears to have widened considerably during the later 1930's, so that a comparison over time with trading profits in other sectors becomes even less meaningful.

The purpose of this study is to examine the comparative results of various types of industrial activity as sources of profit. By taking the figures for trading profits only, we exclude non-trading income earned by the employment of free capital, as having no direct bearing on the *industrial* activity of trading concerns. In any case, distributed profits and debenture interest are both included in the Gross True Income of the enterprises from which they originate. Interest on government securities will not be included anywhere, as it does not represent a return to any kind of industrial activity.

Interpreting the figures of Gross True Income for the Finance group presents two problems. The first is a conceptual one. What is the 'industrial activity' from which a financial enterprise earns its profits? In essence, the activity of finance provides profits out of the difference between the rates for lending and borrowing, or in other words the buying price and the selling price of financial assets. From the economist's point of view, there is no essential difference between a surplus of receipts over costs in the provision of financial services and in the production of any other goods or services. The total commercial profits of financial activity should therefore provide a measure comparable with the trading profits of other activities.

In the particular case of banks, the trading income is earned from the charges made by them for the services provided to their customers. These book-keeping, safe-deposit and general advisory functions must therefore be treated as a specific cost against which bank charges will be offset. If bank charges are deliberately held down below cost for commercial reasons, or if *all* the banks' costs are charged to the 'trading' account, then the 'trading' profit will have little economic significance. The main sources of banking profits are the interest earned on securities and advances. We do not know whether the latter item was treated as trading profit or not, but the former item was treated separately as investment income.

The second problem presented by the Gross True Income figures is that there seems to have been a change, somewhere around 1930, either in the statutory method of assessing profits, or in the policy of financial concerns in switching their source of income. Losses made in trading can be offset against income from interest and dividends. By switching the source of income from that which is paid before tax to that which is paid after tax, the commercial profit may remain unchanged but the loss made in trading can be set off against investment income and lead to a reduced tax liability. The difficulty here is to account for this sudden switching around 1930, which continued till the end of the 1930's. The figures below show how the Gross True Income of British banks fell from a positive £20 m. in 1927 to a value of nearly *minus* £15 m. in 1937. The 'profits' figures are the declared profits of the 23 United Kingdom banks, as published in the 'Economist'. The coverage of the two series of figures is not identical, but the figures of 'profits' will show the general trend of the actual commercial profits in banking.

U.K. BANKS. £ MILLION

		Profits	G.T.I.			Profits	G.T.I.
1927	..	16.5	20.0	1933	..	13.1	
1928	..	17.1		1934	..	13.6	
1929	..	17.3		1935	..	13.6	
1930	..	15.3		1936	..	14.5	−12.6
1931	..	14.0		1937	..	15.2	−14.7
1932	..	13.0	4.5	1938	..	14.4	−12.9

The discrepancy between trading and commercial profits is very obvious in the case of banking, as shown above. The same considerations apply to the other trade groups in Finance, although to a less extent. No useful purpose can be served by including these figures in a comparative study with other sectors of the economy, and they are therefore excluded. For the sake of completeness, the relevant figures are shown separately in the Main Tables, covering banking, insurance and the various classes of broking. Unfortunately, certain commercial services are also included in these trade groups, which one would wish to see in the main body of figures. These include various types of agency engaged in advertising, tourism, entertainment, betting, forwarding and housing, to mention only a few. They are included in the trade group 'Other Brokers and Agents'.

Chapter IV

A TRADE GROUP ANALYSIS OF PROFITS IN THE UNITED KINGDOM

The opening chapter of this study gives ample expression to the qualifications attaching to the figures in our main tables. When all these qualifications have been made it is apparent that our figures do not directly measure any clearly defined quantity. Figures of Gross True Income in any year are not a direct measure of that year's profits in quantities which are relevant to the decisions of a businessman or the studies of an economist. Figures of the numbers of assessments made in a year are even less accurate if viewed as a measure of the number of enterprises operating in that year. Yet it would be tedious to reiterate all the qualifications at every stage of the analysis. It must suffice here to say that when Gross True Income is referred to as profit, the quantities given should be regarded as general orders of magnitude; the margins of error cannot be specified, but will not be such as to render invalid the general conclusions which are drawn from the figures. They are mainly a means of providing fairly reliable comparisons between trade groups or industries in any one year, and to a lesser extent between the same trade group or industry in different years. Similarly, figures for numbers of assessments may be used as though they referred to the numbers of enterprises, but only to give an indication of relative numbers and the relative growth or decline over time.

One of our main tools of analysis, therefore, will be the index number, measuring relative changes over time. The obvious warning should perhaps be given here that the index number gives only an average measure of the change between two years, so that the longer the period between these two years, the less useful the index number will be. For example, a trade group may have doubled its profits between 1909 and 1927 and yet have been in a steady decline for several years past. This deficiency is less formidable in the later years of our series, especially since 1927 was near the peak of a cycle and 1932 near the bottom of a slump. Ignorance of the years in between must, however, set limits to the analysis.

Use may also be made of figures for average profit per enterprise, but even stronger qualifications apply to these. Figures of average profit for corporate concerns are not comparable with those for firms and partnerships. In the latter case, the salaries taken by the proprietors are part of the taxable profits, in the former case the salaries of directors are counted as a deductible cost before tax. On this ground, the average profit of companies should therefore be lower than those of firms and partnerships. The fact that in nearly all cases they are not is due to the considerably larger average size of the corporate concerns. Where the proportion of corporate concerns in a trade group is changing over time, a better indication of trends in average profits is given by figures for corporate and non-corporate concerns separately.

Even then, average profit figures must be treated with caution, especially when the number of assessments shown is small, or when there are likely to be large numbers of non-corporate enterprises earning profits less than the exemption limit. Also, a trade group may be dominated by a handful of very large concerns, with many more very small ones of only minor importance. Railways are a case in point after the setting up of the four main companies in 1921. There were still about a hundred small railway companies in operation, but their share of the total profits was relatively insignificant.

In this chapter we attempt to give an overall picture of the economy in order to reveal the structural changes that occurred, in so far as these are discernible from estimates of profits and numbers of enter-prises. 'Structure' is necessarily a limited concept in this study since our results are not related to a similar study of output or costs. But within the limits of definition of our main terms we are able to show the changing importance of various branches of economic activity.

In the following analysis we are concerned only with the 78 trade groups which have been classified in the following 12 industries: Extraction, Textiles, Metals, Food drink and tobacco, Chemicals, Other manufacturing, Building, Public Utilities, Distribution, Trans-port, Professions and Miscellaneous trades. The Finance group of enterprises is excluded since their profit figures are not on a com-parable basis. These and enterprises operating mainly outside the U.K. are treated elsewhere.

THE PRINCIPAL TRADE GROUPS.

In the succeeding sections of this chapter we shall be examining the performance of individual trade groups over three periods of time. In this section we present a general survey of the main sources of profits in the inter-war period, together with a study of the distribution of enterprises among various activities.

A detailed account of the relative importance of each trade group is given by Main Tables XIV and XV, showing respectively the percentage distribution of Gross True Income and of numbers of assessments for all trade groups in the U.K., but excluding Finance and Agriculture. The data in this section are taken from these tables.

GROSS TRUE INCOME.

Table 1 lists those trade groups which accounted for 2 per cent or more of total profits in 1927 and in 1937. The order of ranking is of course largely dependent upon the fineness of classification. If retail distribution were split into several components, and if various manufacturing activities were combined, a different order would result. Many of the trade groups do, however, represent fairly homogeneous activities, and some generalisations can be made from the available evidence.

TABLE IV.1

Percentage Distribution of Gross True Income in U.K.
Trade Groups with more than 2 per cent of total

1927	Per Cent of G.T.I.	1937	Per Cent of G.T.I.
1. Retail (purely distributive)	13.0	1. Retail (purely distributive)	11.5
2. Retail (semi-industrial)	10.3	2. Wholesale Distribution	8.5
3. Wholesale Distribution	10.0	3. Retail (semi-industrial)	7.6
4. Railways	4.4	4. Machinery, Engineering	5.5
5. Hotels, Inns, etc.	3.5	5. Road Transport	3.9
6. Machinery, Engineering	3.2	6. Shipping	3.7
7. Brewing	3.0	7. Electricity	3.1
8. Medicine and Dentistry	2.9	8. Medicine and Dentistry	2.9
9. Shipping	2.8	9. Railways	2.9
10. Road Transport	2.7	10. Brewing	2.4
11. Law	2.0	11. Hotels, Inns, etc.	2.2
12. Building and Contracting	2.0	12. Coal Mines	2.2
13. Electricity	2.0		

The most notable feature of Table 1 is the importance of the service trades, especially in distribution and transport. Each of the four classified activities comprising the distributive sector are included in both years, with three of them occupying top place. In the transport industry, railways, shipping and road transport appear in both years. In contrast, manufacturing trades are not very evident, although as explained above, this is partly a matter of classification. Machinery and Engineering, Brewing and Electricity appear in both years, the only trade groups to do so out of the total of 53 trade groups in manufacturing industries.

Textiles as a whole accounted for 4.5 per cent of total profits in 1927, and this declined to 3.0 per cent in 1937. The Food trades also declined in importance, from 7.7 per cent to 7.3 per cent, and so did the Other Manufacturing trades, which fell from 8.0 per cent to 7.0 per cent. In Extraction, coal mining increased its share from 1.5 per cent to 2.2 per cent, but this was still well below the 4.6 per cent which it enjoyed in 1909.

It is not possible to calculate the percentage shares of more than a few trades in 1909. Those which we can estimate are:

	%				%
Wholesale Distribution	.. 12.3	Shipping	..	..	.. 4.3
Railways ..	.. .. 12.1	Cotton	..	..	.. 2.3
Coal Mines	.. .. 4.6	Gas	..	..	.. 2.3

A full list of trade groups with over 2 per cent of total profits would also probably include Brewing, Machinery and Engineering, and the three other distributive trades.

It will be noticed that most of the trade groups in the 'top twelve' in 1909 remained there in 1927 and 1937, but sometimes with a considerable change both in the size of their share and in their relative placing. The main newcomers in the 1920's were road transport and electricity, while coal mining, cotton and gas fell from their former eminence.

NUMBERS OF ASSESSMENTS.

In Table 2, ten trade groups are shown as having more than one per cent of the total number of assessments in 1927 and 1932. Not only was the order of size unchanged between these two years, but the individual share of each trade group remained fairly constant. The two retail trades between them accounted for over half of the total number of assessments. The professions also figure prominently, but the only 'manufacturing' trade with over one per cent is Building and Contracting. The ten trades listed accounted for 86 per cent of all assessments in 1927 and 87 per cent in 1937.

TABLE IV.2
Percentage Distribution of Numbers of Assessments in U.K.
Trade Groups with more than 1 per cent of total

					Per Cent of No. of Assts.	
					1927	1937
1.	Retail (purely distributive)	..	..	..	28.9	31.0
2.	Retail (semi-industrial)	..	..	..	23.8	25.1
3.	Misc. profits n.e.s.	..	..	..	8.0	7.6
4.	Hotels, Inns, etc.	..	..	..	7.7	6.1
5.	Wholesale Distribution	..	..	..	5.7	4.9
6.	Other Professions	..	..	..	3.1	3.2
7.	Medicine and Dentistry	..	..	..	3.0	3.1
8.	Road Transport ..	..	..	..	2.9	3.0
9.	Building and Contracting ..	..	..	..	1.7	1.8
10.	Law ..	..	..	..	1.2	1.2

If a comparable list were drawn up for 1909 all ten of these trades would be included, though with some large differences in the size of their share. Retail (semi-industrial) then accounted for 11.9 per cent of the total, compared with 23.8 per cent in 1927. Hotels and Inns comprised 11.6 per cent in 1909, but in 1927 their proportion had fallen to 7.7 per cent. There were also six other trades, with more than one per cent of the total number of assessments. These were Professional engineers and architects, Literature and Art, Markets and Tolls, Music and Drama, Quarries and Printing.

Summarizing the data in Tables 1 and 2 above, one can say that the principal sources of profit, in the aggregate, and the majority of enterprises during the inter-war period were in those activities providing distributive, transport and certain professional services. Unlike most of the trade groups excluded from Tables 1 and 2, these are activities which are undertaken in all areas of population, and in which the service is generally rendered directly to the final consumer.

The analysis now proceeds chronologically in three phrases: 1909–27, 1927–32, 1932–36/38.

I.   1909–1927

In Main Tables XII and XIII index numbers for profits and numbers of assessments are given for each trade group and industry for each year of the series, using 1927 as base year. The movements of these index numbers, for each of the industrial totals (and sub-totals within Manufacturing) are shown diagrammatically in Charts I and II. With certain exceptions, the basic pattern of change in profits and numbers was very similar between 1909 and 1927. In round numbers

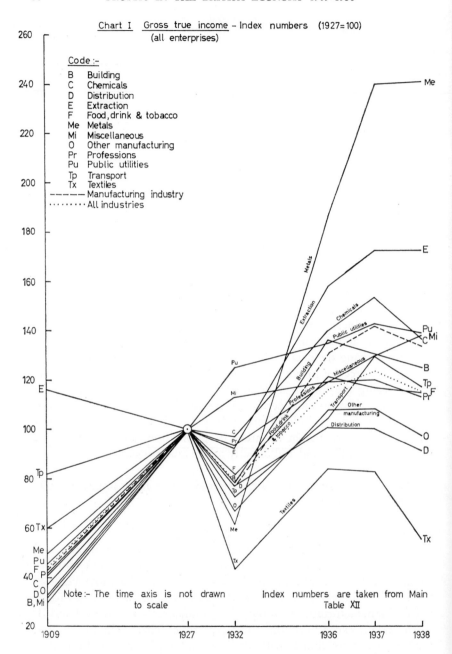

Chart I   Gross true income – Index numbers (1927=100)
(all enterprises)

Code :–
B   Building
C   Chemicals
D   Distribution
E   Extraction
F   Food, drink & tobacco
Me   Metals
Mi   Miscellaneous
O   Other manufacturing
Pr   Professions
Pu   Public utilities
Tp   Transport
Tx   Textiles
––––––– Manufacturing industry
·········· All industries

Note :– The time axis is not drawn to scale

Index numbers are taken from Main Table XII

profits rose from £370 m. to £840 m., and the assessments made rose from 400,000 to 1,030,000. The index for profits in 1909 is 44 and for assessments 39.

If we examine this growth in terms of the industrial groups we see the similarity in the growths of profits and numbers. The exceptions to this are in Extraction, Transport and Public Utilities. Excluding these for the time being, the range of values of index numbers for the

Chart II   Number of assessments – Index numbers   (1927=100)
(all enterprises)

Code :-

B	Building
C	Chemicals
D	Distribution
E	Extraction
F	Food,drink & tobacco
Me	Metals
Mi	Miscellaneous
O	Other manufacturing
Pr	Professions
Pu	Public utilities
Tp	Transport
Tx	Textiles
– – – –	Manufacturing industry
········	All industries

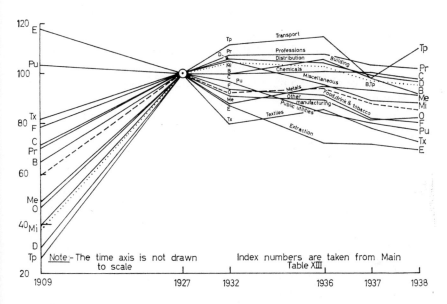

Note:- The time axis is not drawn to scale

Index numbers are taken from Main Table XIII

E

other nine industries is 30 to 60 for profits and 31 to 82 for numbers. The rates of increase of the two sets of values also show a fair degree of correspondence.

It appears then that the years 1909 to 1927 were on balance a period of considerable growth for most of the economy, with increasing profits being matched by the appearance of new enterprises. In total, the profits in the 9 industries increased by 170 per cent and the number of assessments increased by 160 per cent.

A trade group analysis of the 9 industries shows the same absence of any marked differences in performance, with most trade groups making similar advances in profits and numbers over this 18 year period. Figures for Gross True Income in 1909 are not available individually for many trade groups, but one or two can be selected for special mention.

The largest recorded rate of increase in profit occurred in tobacco manufacture, where it rose from £2.8 m. to £12.2 m. Profits in retailing, including the hotel trade, also rose considerably, from £54 m. to £225 m. In tobacco, increased profits were secured with no significant increase in total numbers, but with a shift from non-corporate to corporate organisation. Average profits increased considerably. In retail trading, there was a corresponding increase in the number of assessments so that the average profit remained at the same level. This increase was of the order of 450,000.[1]

At the other end of the scale, none of the trades for which we have figures in these nine industries showed a decline in profits. The smallest rates of advance were in the cotton and wool trades, each of which had an increase of about £3 m., to £11.9 m. and £8.8 m. respectively. The total number of enterprises engaged in these two trades showed a small net increase despite the noticeable disappearance of the small firm or partnership. None of the larger trade groups showed an unusual increase or decrease in numbers, apart from retailing mentioned above.

Our review so far has covered nine industries with a total of 65 trade groups. It is not the intention to enter into a detailed analysis of each trade group, but only to depict the salient points of the outline and select the exceptional cases for comment. The basic data are contained in the main tables, and if comment is brief it is because there is little of exception upon which to comment. An analysis of the trade groups within the nine 'normal' industries reveals little that is not consistent with the broader industrial analysis.

[1] But see Chapter I, pp. 23, 24.

The other three industries, Extraction, Public Utilities and Transport, stand out as exceptions to the general pattern of growth. We turn to these now, and isolate the trade groups which showed the most pronounced trends.

EXTRACTION

This was the only industry in which profits showed a net decline over the period 1909 to 1927. The decline was mainly due to the heavy fall shown for coal mining profits, which dropped from £17 m. to £12 m. This apparent fall was probably due mainly to losses brought forward from 1926, the year of the coal strike. The gross assessments for coal mines in 1909 and 1927 were £18.3 m. and £18.0 m. respectively. Even this latter figure may be influenced by some results for 1926. Owing to the spread of accounting years within the industry about a sixth of the total assessment would relate to 1926. Figures of output may give a better picture of performance. Output of coal in the U.K. was 251 million tons in 1927, compared with an annual average of 263 million tons in the three years 1908–10. In 1926 output was only 126 million tons.

Profits in iron and other mining showed a negligible drop, and in quarrying a normal growth. However, the small actual increase in quarrying profits, from £1.2 m. to £3.4 m., was in contrast to the change in numbers of enterprises. The number of assessments fell from 4,130 to 3,150, with the result that the average profit per enterprise rose steeply from about £300 to over £1,000. This was in conjunction with a movement of numbers from the non-corporate to the corporate sphere; but quarrying remained an activity carried on predominantly by a large number of small enterprises.

The number of enterprises engaged in iron and other mining also declined, but this activity was relatively unimportant. Coal mining, although the establishments were fewer in number than in quarrying, remained in each of the six years the only important source of profits in the industry. In the years 1909 to 1927, the net increase in numbers was relatively small. The number of non-corporate coal mines remained the same, at around 600, and the larger enterprises increased by about 200 to a total of about 1,000. Later years show a marked decline in numbers of both large and small units although, as we shall see later, rationalisation was accompanied by a substantial increase in profits, both total and average.

PUBLIC UTILITIES

As a whole, public utilities combined a normal profit growth with a fall in the number of enterprises. Profits rose from £19 m. to £41 m., with the number of assessments falling from 4,780 to 4,600. In this respect it was the only industry of its kind in the period. However, the industry totals conceal certain trade group differences which are of interest.

The greatest profit increase was in the new electricity industry. Profits increased fourfold, from £4.1 m. to £16.5 m. Numbers rose at a slightly slower rate than the average, from 490 to 1,040. In contrast to this, the numbers engaged in gas and water undertakings fell, from 1,630 to 1,500 and from 2,670 to 2,070 respectively. Electricity also showed less sign of concentration than the other two, about a fifth of its numbers being non-corporate, as opposed to only about a ninth in gas and water concerns.

Profits in gas and water increased, although in the latter case the rise was relatively small. More significant is the fact that in each of these three trade groups the average profit per enterprise was more or less doubled while in the economy as whole the average fell by about 10 per cent.

Finally, we may note the interesting comparison that gas and electricity profits combined rose by £20 m. over a period when coal mining had shown a fall of £5 m.

TRANSPORT

Excluding the extractive industry, where profits fell, the transport industry had the smallest rate of growth in profits of any of the other eleven industries. At the same time, the numbers of assessments suggest that the increase in enterprises was at a higher rate than in any other industry. The figures are £73 m. to £90 m. for profits, and 8,790 to 32,220 for numbers. Here again, though, important differences emerge from a trade group analysis.

In shipping, profits rose rather less than the average, to a level of £24 m. Numbers, on the other hand, fell by a greater amount than in any other trade group, from 3,930 to 2,440. This fall was almost equally evident in both the corporate and non-corporate sectors, suggesting a decided trend towards concentration. The average profit per shipping enterprise increased by over three times.

Railway profits were another rare example (with coal mining) of a substantial decrease in this period. They fell from £45 m. to £37 m.[1] The number of railway companies also declined, largely due to the formation of the four main lines after the 1921 Act. Assessments recorded fell from 172 to 112. Rationalisation may have mitigated the effects of the General Strike, the Depression and the enormous increase in the use of road transport throughout the period, but profits never again approached the 1909 figure of £45 m.

Road transport showed the most spectacular rate of increase in numbers of any trade group in this period, rising from 4,150 to 30,160. Also, this increase was faster in the non-corporate than in the corporate sector, the number of the former rising from 3,390 to 27,580. Profits too rose faster than the national average, from £7 m. to £23 m. but this was by no means commensurate with the increase in numbers. The average profit in 1927 was less than half the 1909 average. The evidence therefore suggests a proliferation of successful but small-scale enterprises in road transport.

We see now that the figures for the transport industry as a whole conceal very divergent trends among the main trade groups. Compared with the average rate of increase in profits in the whole economy, road transport profits showed an exceptional rise and railway profits showed an exceptional fall. The increase in shipping profits was rather less than average. A similar comparison for numbers of enterprises shows road transport making an exceptional rise, with shipping and railways both undergoing an exceptional contraction. The two main competing forms of land transport, road and rail, showed a relatively modest combined increase, from £52 m. to £60 m.

The period under review saw the exploitation of the internal combustion engine. Unfortunately, a separate figure for the profits of the Motor and Cycle trade group in 1909 cannot be given, but the 1927 figure of £9.6 m., suggests a possible increase of about £8 m. or £9 m. since 1909. It is interesting to note that the increase in road transport profits was double this amount.

To summarize the main features of the period 1909 to 1927:

(i) Profits in 1927 were two and a quarter times their 1909 level; numbers were two and a half times their 1909 level. There were only a few trade groups which deviated widely from these mean rates of increase.

---

[1] These figures are net of a certain amount for repairs and maintenance. See Ch. I, p. 11.

(ii) The highest rates of increase in total profits occurred in the following trade groups: Tobacco, retail trading, electricity, road transport and some of the miscellaneous (and probably newer) manufacturing and service trades. A substantial fall in profits occurred only in coal mining and railways. The two main textile groups, cotton and wool, increased their profits only slightly.

(iii) The highest rates of increase in numbers of assessments occurred in the following trade groups: Road transport, retail trading, sugar and glucose, and tinplate. The main trades which declined in numbers were shipping, railways, lace, quarrying, waterworks and gasworks.

II. 1927–1932

The figures of Gross True Income in 1932 give an indication of the effects of the Depression on profit levels as compared with 1927. This was a crucial period for the economy, in which not only did profits fall drastically, but in which the distribution of profits showed radical changes. It was in certain respects an important turning point, and we shall explore it rather more fully than the other periods.

In 1932, the total profits of the 78 trade groups stood at £664 m., a drop of 21 per cent from the 1927 level of £840 m. The decreases in the corporate and non-corporate sectors were 20.7 per cent and 21.4 per cent respectively. It is doubtful whether much significance should be attached to the near equality of these average values, for they conceal wide differences of value between the various trade groups in each sector. For one thing, there was greater variation in the movements of the profits of the corporate trade groups, of which 24 increased or maintained their total profits over this period as opposed to only seven non-corporate groups. Further, in none of the subsequent years of our series did the total profits of the non-corporate sector regain their 1927 level. It is possible, therefore, that in 1932 there was already a secular trend operating to depress the profits of firms and partnerships relative to the others, concurrent with the cyclical movement which was depressing all profits. On the other hand, it may be that the Depression itself effected a change in the organisational structure of British industry, leaving the advantage to the larger and stronger enterprises in the period of recovery. Speculation cannot be pushed too far, but it seems likely that different influences were at work to produce this almost identical drop in profits in the corporate and non-corporate groups.

Before looking at the results for 1932, it will be as well to set them in the perspective of the whole period covered by this report. The most striking difference between the periods before and after 1927 is shown by the relative movement of the index numbers of Gross True Income and number of assessments. (See Charts I and II). We have seen how for the period 1909 to 1927 both these series of index numbers were broadly similar in both average value and range, denoting a fairly uniform growth throughout most of the economy. The behaviour of these index numbers after 1927 is very different.

On the one hand, the changes in profits of the twelve industries showed a very wide range of variation, with the range increasing year by year. The ranges of profit index numbers for the 12 industries in 1932 and the last three years are 81, 103, 158 and 186 points respectively. If trade group values are taken, the range in 1938 is seen to approach 500 points; in 1932 the spread was 130 points and in 1909 it was 120 points. This implies an ever increasing divergence in the rate of growth of earnings in the different types of activity.

On the other hand, the relative constancy of the number of assessments made over the period 1927 to 1938 suggests that the number of enterprises operating in each industry changed very little.[1] The high tide mark in fact comes in 1932 in our series, with 1,076,500 assessments recorded for that year. After that, there is a gradual but continuing decline. The ranges of index numbers of the number of assessments for the twelve industries from 1932 onwards are 32, 43, 31 and 42 points respectively. If trade group values are taken there is the same picture of mainly very small rates of change, much of which cannot be regarded as very significant, given the approximate nature of the figures.

The change in numbers, as in profits, followed a different course in the corporate and non-corporate spheres. The turning point for firms and partnerships came in 1932, with a total of 992,500. Five years later there were 10 per cent less, whereas the corporate concerns had by this time increased in number by about 25 per cent, to a total of 103,500. The encroachment of companies and municipal corporations into activities previously carried on by firms and partnerships continued throughout the inter-war period and is reflected alike in relative profits and numbers of enterprises.

---

[1] The nominal exemption limit was lower in 1932 than in 1927, but the effective exemption limit may have been higher. See Ch. I, p. 14.

Turning now to the experiences of individual trade groups in 1932, it is seen that the effect of the Depression on profit levels was very uneven. Twenty-one of the 78 trade groups had profits in 1932 equal to or greater than their profits in 1927,[1] while a further four were less than 10 per cent down. The profits of half of the 78 trade groups fell by between 20 per cent and 50 per cent, and in six cases profits fell by more than 60 per cent. The overall total was down by 21 per cent.

If we take a profit index number of 100 or over (1927=100) as a mark of success in 1932, only two of the twelve industries emerge as 'successful'. These were Public Utilities (125 per cent) and Miscellaneous trades (113 per cent). Next in order came Chemicals (97 per cent), Professions (94 per cent) and Extraction (92 per cent). The incidence of success among the 22 trade groups included in these five industries was very irregular. Only 11 of them were 'successful'. Again, the six trades with the highest rate of profit increase were each in a different industry as classified here. It is difficult to find any common factor or factors to which one can relate performance in this period. From the information available however, it is worth investigating four lines of enquiry, as follows:

(i) With a considerable drop in the level of total demand, one may find a change in the structure of demand, reflected in the relative earnings of different activities. For example, one expects consumer trades to weather a depression more successfully than heavy industry.

(ii) Trades which relied to a large extent on export markets may have faced greater difficulties than those which produced mainly for the home market.

(iii) A change in the number of enterprises may be related (either as cause or effect) to the ability to maintain profit growth. Also the degree of corporate organisation may have been a factor of strength.

(iv) An increase in the capital employed in industry may have led, through higher productivity, to a higher gross income, whatever the effect unused capacity may have had on the percentage yield on total capital. On this point we are particularly handicapped in having no direct measure of capital assets, and the most we can do is to use the figures of depreciation allowances as a very approximate indicator for seeing where the major changes in capital occurred.

To facilitate the discussion of the questions outlined above, the 78 trade groups are divided into two classes. The 21 trade groups whose Gross True Income in 1932 was equal to or greater than their 1927

[1] This includes two trade groups in which profits had fallen by less than half per cent.

income are called 'A' groups. The 57 remaining trade groups whose gross income fell over this period are called 'B' groups. A comparison is then made of the A and B groups in respect of their changes in other factors, namely Average Gross True Income, Number of Assessments, Wear and Tear Allowances, and Net True Income. Some of these are given for corporate and non-corporate concerns separately. Changes in these factors are described, in the same way, as being either 'a' or 'b', denoting respectively an increase (or no change) or a decrease on the 1927 value.

Table 3 sets out the 21 A groups, in descending order of percentage increase of Gross True Income, and shows for each of them the direction of change in the above quantities. For ease of reading, only the 'a' changes are noted, the downward changes ('b') being left blank. The comparison of the A and B groups at the bottom of the table is designed to show as simply as possible the extent of the concurrence of an expansion in profits with a change in other factors.

(i) *The Sources of profit.*

The 21 A groups come from nine of our twelve industries. The three industries which contained no A groups were Textiles, Distribution and Building.

The industry which fared best in this period was Public Utilities. Total profits for these three trade groups increased by 25 per cent, from £41 m. to £51 m. The average profit for the industry increased from £8,800 to £11,350. Although gas profits fell by 5 per cent, this was more than offset by the 55 per cent rise in electricity profits. Thus the provision of power and light and water remained a profitable service despite the setback in economic activity.

Profits from coal mining also increased by 4 per cent, but in actual amount this was only about £500,000. Output of coal in this period had, however, fallen considerably, from 251 m. tons in 1927 to 209 m. tons in 1932.[1] It is possible that the recorded increase in profit was more apparent than real, due to the artificially low figure for 1927.

In the field of services generally, profits seem to have been more stable than in the production of goods. The professions as a whole dropped by 6 per cent, mainly on account of a setback in Law and in Engineering and Architecture. With the latter case we may note the fall of 21 per cent in the profits of the building trades. Accountancy, Medicine, and Music and Drama all gained. Entertainment in fact

[1] But see p. 59.

was one of the more profitable activities in 1932—Public Amusements were up 24 per cent.

The distributive services on the other hand suffered large absolute falls in profit, totalling £73 m. for the four trade groups, a drop of 23 per cent. The numbers of such enterprises continued to increase, however, and in 1932 retail units numbered 588,000–47,000 more assessments than in 1927.

The effect of the depression on profits in transport services was very varied. Docks and canals and Road Transport increased their profit by 9 per cent and 8 per cent respectively, but the railways had a 36 per cent decrease and in shipping the fall in profits was as much as 60 per cent. The latter can be explained largely by the shrinking of foreign trade. In the case of the railways, the decline was partly a result of the fall in industrial activity, and partly the effect of the increasing competition from road transport. The following figures indicate the extent of this movement.

	1928	1932
(a) Railway passenger train receipts £m	82	67
(b) Railway goods train receipts £m.	103	81
(c) Railways' Net Revenue £m.	42	27
(d) Number of private cars ('000)	885	1,128
(e) Number of road goods vehicles ('000)	306	370
(f) Index of Industrial Production (1924=100)	105.5	93.3
Gross True Income Railways £m.	37[1]	24
,, Road Transport £m. ..	23[1]	25

[1] Refers to 1927.
Sources: (a), (b), (c) and (f) Statistical Abstract for the U.K. (d) and (e) Basic Road Statistics.

Looking at the totals of manufacturing industry there is a suggestion that on average the consumer trades maintained their profits rather more successfully than heavy industry. The main exception is in the textile trades, where one can see a secular decline at work. Textile profits as a percentage of the six annual totals were respectively, 6.1, 4.5, 2.5, 3.2, 3.0, and 2.1. It was only in hosiery and miscellaneous textiles that profits ever regained their 1927 level in our subsequent years. A downward trend was also apparent in the clothing and footwear trade groups.

In the category of general manufacturing, mostly concerned with the production of consumer goods, only paper-making and the unspecified, miscellaneous trades showed an increase in profits. The latter will to a certain extent include the new and growing trades whose

TABLE IV.3   1927–1932

I. Analysis of the twenty-one 'A' trade groups, whose Gross True Income in 1932 was at least as great as in 1927.
II. Comparison with the fifty-seven 'B' trade groups, whose Gross True Income in 1932 was lower than in 1927

I The A Groups	1932 G.T.I. £mn.	Percent increase on 1927	Gross True Income		Average Gross True Income		Number of Assessments			Wear & Tear	Net True Income
			C	N.C.	C	N.C.	All	C	N.C.	All	All
Telephones	.3	171	a	..	a	..	a	a	..	a	a
Grain Milling	4.3	60	a		a	a	a	a		a	a
Electricity	25.5	55	a	a	a		a	a	a	a	a
Paper-making	5.5	39	a		a		a	a		a	a
Lead, Tin, Zinc	1.7	27	a		a		a	a		a	a
Public Amusements	8.7	24	a		a					a	a
Water	10.4	20	a		a		a	a	a	a	a
Misc. profits n.e.s.	16.5	14	a	a	a	a	a	a	a	a	a
Tinplate	.7	12	a		a					a	
Fine Chemicals	9.1	10	a		a		a	a	a	a	a
Docks, Canals	6.0	9	a		a					a	
Road Transport	24.9	8	a		a		a	a	a	a	a
Manufactures n.e.s.	4.7	7	a		a					a	
Accountancy	8.4	5	a	a	a		a	a	a	a	a
Coal Mines	12.7	4	a		a					a	
Fertilizers, Explosives	9.9	3	a		a					a	
Music and Drama	2.3	2	a	a	a		a	a	a	a	a
Medicine and Dentistry	24.2	1	a	a	a		a	a	a	a	a
Misc. Metals	.6	—	a								
Markets, Tolls	1.6	—	a							a	
Misc. Foods	7.5	—	a		a	a				a	
II All A groups: a:			21	5	19	3	12	12	8	20	13
b:			—	15	2	17	9	9	12	1	8
All B groups: a:			3	2	5	3	11	23	7	39	—
b:			54	53	52	52	46	34	48	18	57

Notes. C.=corporate enterprises. N.C.=non-corporate enterprises.
The letter 'a' in a column denotes an increase, or no change, or a decrease of less than 0.5 per cent, in the quantity signified at the head of that column. The letter 'b' denotes a decrease in the quantity. In part I, the 'b' cells have been left blank. Owing to the virtual exclusion of Telephones, Railways and Combines of engineering, etc., from the non-corporate sector, this contains only 20 A groups and 55 B groups.

activities did not fit into the existing categories. Vacuum cleaners, domestic machines, patent fuel and linoleum are examples of this. In total, the Other Manufacturing group suffered a fall in profits of exactly one-third.

The metal trades group, containing heavy industry, was even less successful. Profits were 39 per cent down. The largest percentage fall was in shipbuilding, which dropped from £1.4 m. to £0.4 m. There were some very heavy absolute falls in profit in this industry. Machinery and Engineering fell by £12 m., Motor and Cycle by £4.1 m., Wrought Iron by £2.3 m. and Iron and Steel by £1.9 m. Three of the smaller trade groups managed to maintain or increase their profits, both total and average. They were Lead, Tin and Zinc, Tinplate, and Misc. Metals. But their combined profit increase was only £400,000.

After public utilities, the chemical industry was the next most successful of the manufacturing sector. But here it was in the field of industrial chemicals that profits advanced. For Patent Medicines and Soap and Candles, total profits fell by about a quarter.

The food, drink and tobacco trades showed great variations in performance. Sugar and Glucose, for instance, fell by 48 per cent, while Grain Milling rose by 61 per cent, and Misc. Foods remained at the same level. Profits in the drink trades fell, although the average profit in distilling rose slightly.

From the above brief description of the situation in 1932, it seems that no obvious generalisations can be made as to the relation between changes in profits and changes in the structure of demand. There is evidence of increasing profitability in public utilities and professional and entertainment services, but not in distribution or transport. There is also no convincing evidence of a clear cut distinction between the performance of consumer trades and heavy industry, although there appears to be a bias in favour of the former.

No doubt the influence of demand was strong, but there were probably other factors, on the supply side, working in various ways to offset the effects on the final profit levels.

(ii) *Exports*.

One factor which may have affected profits in certain trade groups during the period is the decline in world demand for our exports. The total f.o.b. value of exports, exclusive of re-exports, was as follows:

1927: £709 m.	1930: £571 m.
1928: £724 m.	1931: £391 m.
1929: £729 m.	1932: £365 m.

Exports in 1932 were 48.5 per cent lower than in 1927; in the same period profits fell by 21 per cent. The question is, did our major exporting trades suffer a larger or smaller setback in profits during this period?

Table 4 compares changes in profits and exports for certain trades. The two series of figures are by no means exactly comparable. The export figures are taken from the U.K. Annual Statements of Trade, with a classification in some cases very different from that used in the profits enquiry. Only those trades are shown in our table where the export classes and our trade groups match reasonably well. Also, the export values, being f.o.b., include returns to transport and other services, but this should not invalidate any measure of change between the two years.

TABLE IV.4
Profits and Exports. £ million

Trade group[1]	Profits[2] 1927	Profits[2] 1932	Exports[2] 1927	Exports[2] 1928	Exports[2] 1932
1. (E) Coal	12.2	12.7	45.5		31.6
2. (E_1) Cotton	11.9	3.3	148.8		62.8
3. (E_1) Wool	8.8	4.9	56.8		24.0
4. (E_1) All other textile trades	16.7	8.1	29.5		14.2
5. (E_2) Iron and steel; Anchor, Chain; Wrought iron, etc.; Tinplate	12.1	7.9	69.4		28.0
6. (E_2) Machinery, engineering	27.1	15.1	61.8		35.3
7. (E_2) Shipbuilding	1.4	.4	4.5	15.9	3.9
8. (E_2) Rly. carriage and wagon	1.1	.6	9.2		1.4
9. (E_2) Motor and cycle	9.6	5.5	20.6		13.7
10. Copper, brass; lead, tin, zinc	3.6	3.0	19.9		6.9
11. Grain milling	2.7	4.3	5.6		3.3
12. Brewing	24.8	18.9	1.5		1.1
13. (E_3) Tobacco	12.2	10.2	8.4		4.2
14. All other food and drink trades	25.4	19.7	36.8		23.7
15. (E_3) Patent medicines	1.0	.8	3.0		2.6
16. All other chemical trades	23.4	23.0	20.4		14.7
17. Leather and rubber	8.5	4.5	11.6		4.9
18. Boots and shoes	3.9	2.3	4.8		2.5
19. Misc. clothing	10.4	5.8	21.0		9.3
20. Paper	4.0	5.5	9.1		6.5
21. (E_3) Pottery	1.4	.9	6.3		3.0
22. (E_3) Glass	1.6	1.1	2.3		1.3
23. (E_3) Instruments	5.5	2.7	8.8		5.5
Total of above trades	229	161	569		281
Total of all trades in U.K. (excluding Finance)	840	664	709		365

[1] Trade groups prefixed by the letter 'E' refer to those which exported more than 10 per cent of total output. (See text on p. 71).

[2] 'Profits' are the Gross True Income of the trade groups listed in the left hand column. Exports are taken from the U.K. Annual Statements of Trade and refer to classes of goods more or less comparable with the outputs of the profits trade groups. (See text on p. 70).

It has been possible to ascribe about four-fifths of total exports to the trade groups shown in Table 4. The selected exports fell from £569 m. to £281 m., a drop of 51 per cent. Profits in the corresponding trade groups fell from £229 m. to £161 m., a drop of 30 per cent. This compares with a fall in profits of 17 per cent in the six of our classified industries not directly engaged in exporting, namely: building, public utilities, distribution, transport, the professions and the miscellaneous trades.

This difference cannot of course be explained solely in terms of exports. In a closed economy one might expect the manufacturing and service trades to fare differently during a depression, solely through changes in the pattern of demand. In a trading nation, on the other hand, the export trades might fare better if overseas demand did not fall to the same extent as home demand. This, of course, was not the case in 1932, when foreign trade in many commodities had fallen to a greater extent than home trade.

The export classes taken from the Statements of Trade, numbered according to the trade group column, are as follows:

Trade group number	Export class number	Description of goods
1.	II A	Coal
2.	III I	Cotton yarns and manufactures
3.	III J	Woollen and worsted yarns and manufactures
4.	III K	Silk yarns and manufactures
	III L	Manufactures of other textile materials
5.	III C	Iron and steel and manufactures thereof
6.	III G	Machinery
	III F	Electrical goods and apparatus
7.	III R (pt)	Ships and boats (new)
8.	III R (pt)	Rail vehicles
9.	III R (pt)	Road vehicles
10.	III D	Non-ferrous metals and manufactures thereof
11.	I A	Grain and flour
12.	I F (pt)	Beer and ale
13.	I G	Tobacco
14.	I (rest)	Food, drink and tobacco
15.	III N (pt)	Drugs, medicines and medicinal preparations
16.	III N (rest)	Chemicals, drugs, dyes and colours
17.	III P	Leather and manufactures thereof
	III S	Rubber manufactures
18.	III M (pt)	Boots and shoes
19.	III M (rest)	Apparel
20.	III Q	Paper, cardboard, etc.
21.	III B (pt)	Pottery and other clay products
22.	III B (pt)	Glass and glassware
23.	III E	Cutlery, hardware, implements and instruments

It can be seen that most of the trade groups listed in Table 4 suffered fairly heavy percentage falls in profit. The only exceptions are coal, grain milling, other chemical trades, and paper. All trades, however, appear to have suffered large falls in exports.

As a determinant of profits, the important factor is not so much the total quantity exported, and the decline in this quantity, but the proportion which the value of exports represents of total output.

The only source of information on the production and exports of different trades is the 1930 Census of Production, and this presents two major difficulties. Exports are measured in a variety of ways: by weights, quantities, or f.o.b. values, or not at all. Secondly, the Census introduces yet another system of classification. Nevertheless, there are certain trades where the two classifications fit fairly closely, and where it is obvious that well over 10 per cent of total output was exported in 1930. These trades are marked in Table 4 by the letter E. In other words, an export ratio of 10 per cent of output has been taken as the defining feature of an 'Exporting' trade, and by excluding doubtful or borderline cases any difference that may be found in profit changes between these trades and others is deliberately under-stated.

Amongst the Exporting trades, coal appears to have been subject to exceptional circumstances. Profits rose slightly and exports did not fall by as much as the average. If we exclude coal, the other Exporting trades fall into three general categories: Textiles; metal trades, producing mainly capital goods; other manufacturing trades, producing mainly consumer goods. In Table 4, these have been marked E_1, E_2, E_3 respectively. In total, the exports of these E trades accounted for 60 per cent of all U.K. exports in 1927, and 55 per cent in 1932.

Table 5 shows the changes in profits and exports of these three categories.

TABLE IV.5
The 'Exporting' Trades

				1927	1932	*Per cent fall*
				£m.	£m.	
E_1	Textiles	..	.. Profits	37	16	56
			Exports	235	101	57
E_2	Metals	..	.. Profits	51	30	42
			Exports	166	82	50
E_3	Others	..	.. Profits	22	16	28
			Exports	29	17	42
	Total of above ..		.. Profits	110	62	44
			Exports	429	200	53

By combining the trades into these three groups the imprecision from using two systems of classification becomes less serious. It is also possible to discern some interesting differences between our three classes of export.

Exports of the E trades fell by 53 per cent, compared with a fall in total exports of 49 per cent. Capital goods, for which demand had fallen especially low during the depression, accounted for a large proportion of total exports. These fell by 50 per cent. Textiles also formed a large proportion of our exports, 33 per cent in 1927 and 28 per cent in 1932. We have seen already how the secular decline in demand for textiles was accentuated by the depression. The exports of the category of 'Others' fell by 42 per cent, which is rather less than the average. This may be partly due to the method of selecting the E trades; it was not possible to obtain such a good 'fit' between the Census and profits trade groups in this category.

Profits in the E trades fell by 44 per cent. This appears to be considerably more than the average fall. Table 4 shows that those trade groups which accounted for about 80 per cent of total exports suffered a fall in profits of 30 per cent. The profit fall in our six non-export industries was 17 per cent.

Table 5 shows that in the three E groups listed, the percentage fall in exports is positively associated with the percentage fall in profits. Textiles suffered most in both, metals were second in both, and the others in E_3 were considerably more fortunate. It will be seen that this is also the ranking order for size of exports; it is also probably the order for ratio of exports to production.

This brief detour into the experience of our export trades has necessarily been limited in scope and technique. The data presented here do not justify any assertion as to the amount by which profits were diminished by loss of export markets. It does indicate, though, that the greater the reliance on exports, the greater the fall in profits was likely to be. Whether this was due to the general decline in world trade, or to the fact that our exports were predominantly textile and metal manufactures, is outside the scope of this study. Both factors were obviously relevant. The important point for the export trades was that they were not able to supplement their decreased earnings overseas with higher profits at home.

(iii) *The Number of Enterprises.*

The aim of this section is to see whether there is any connection between the ability of a trade group to maintain or increase profits through the depression, and a change in the number of enterprises operating in that trade group. Also, we compare the relative numbers of corporate and non-corporate concerns to see whether the type of organisation had any significance.

In most trade groups, and especially in manufacturing, one might expect this distinction to be associated with the size of the concern, large scale operations being carried on by companies while the firms and partnerships are engaged in only small scale operations. While this may be true in a general sense over a large part of industry, it can here be no more than supposition, more valid for some trade groups than for others. There will also be factors other than size which determine the extent of incorporation, and the corporate sector may contain many very small scale concerns alongside the giant companies and corporations. The figures for average profit per enterprise do suggest, however, that the average company conducted a considerably larger business than the average firm or partnership in nearly all fields of activity, and that the difference between the two was widening during the inter-war period.

What we find is that the A groups tended to increase in number more than the B groups. Only 9 of the 21 A groups fell in number, compared with 46 of the 57 B groups. Most of the increase occurred in the corporate sphere: of the A groups, 12 rose and 9 fell; of the B groups 23 rose and 34 fell. Among non-corporate trade groups, only 8 A groups and 7 B groups increased in number.

Nothing very definite emerges from these figures. It is evident though that the non-corporate firms had declined in importance, and that they declined rather more rapidly in the activities where profits contracted. Further, there is a suggestion that the numbers of corporate concerns increased more rapidly in the more profitable activities. It may be that, where opportunities were found to exist, they were seized more successfully by the larger enterprises, with the small man either going out of business or incorporating with others.

The profit figures show that the 21 A groups achieved their success almost entirely through the performance of the corporate enterprises. All 21 showed increases in corporate profits, while only five of them also had increases in the non-corporate sector. These five were in public utilities and the professions, and the total increase was negligible.

The decision to enter a certain field of activity will depend on the number already engaged in that activity, as well as on the total profits deriving from it; *i.e.* on the profitability for the individual firm. The figures in this study give no more than a rough guide as to where

F

some of the opportunities for profit making may have occurred. Our classification of activities is broad, and the quantities derived for average profit may conceal important variations. However, it is of interest to observe the relation between changes in numbers and changes in average profit in both the A and B trade groups.

Taking all enterprises together, 17 of the A groups maintained or increased the level of their average profit over this period. Eight of them increased in number, and none of them decreased. The four trade groups which showed a lower average profit all increased in number, the main one being road transport. Only three of the B groups had a higher average profit, these being Anchor and Chain, Distilling and Gas. Overall, then, the relatively greater increase in numbers of the A groups compared with the B groups was more than offset by their increase in total profits, with the result that in most cases the average profit in the A groups was not brought down by the entry of new enterprises.

Amongst the B groups the reverse happened. In spite of the fact that the number of enterprises appeared to contract in 46 trade groups, out of the total of 57, this was not sufficient to offset the greater contraction in total profits. The average profit fell in 54 of these trade groups.

A more clear cut distinction appears if the corporate and non-corporate concerns are taken separately. With two minor exceptions, and despite a tendency for numbers to increase, all the corporate A groups emerged with a higher average profit, as opposed to only 5 of the B groups. In the non-corporate field, only 3 A groups and 3 B groups had a higher average profit. In fact there was practically no significant increase in average profit in any non-corporate activity.[1]

In conclusion, one may venture the opinion that the profitable activities of the A groups were not over populated with enterprises, and that the B groups were. Furthermore, these profitable activities were almost exclusively the province of the companies and corporations. The average firm or partnership was nowhere fully able to meet the depressed conditions of 1932, whatever the success of his larger competitors may have been.

(iv) *Wear and Tear.*

The total depreciation allowances for all 78 trade groups in 1932 was £11.7 m. higher than the 1927 total, having risen from £70 m. to

[1] The reader is referred again to the difficulty of interpreting these figures (pp. 23, 24, 30).

£82 m.[1] Taking the A groups alone, the total was up by £13 m. This means that although only 18 B groups were granted less against wear and tear, the increased amounts of the other 39 B groups were insufficient to offset this, leaving a net decrease of £1.3 m.

With one minor exception, all A groups had higher wear and tear allowances, and in four groups the increase was substantial. Electricity rose from £4.4 m. to £8.5 m., road transport from £6.4 m. to £9.4 m., coal mining from £1.5 m. to £3.6 m., and fine chemicals from £0.9 m. to £2.0 m.

Although the general difference between the A and B groups is very noticeable, it is hard to particularise in individual cases. There were considerable increases in wear and tear in some of the B groups. For instance, combines of heavy engineering concerns increased their wear and tear from £0.4 m. to £1.2 m.; gas undertakings increased theirs from £1.4 m. to £2.1 m., while the two retail groups together increased theirs from £3.7 m. to £7.0 m. However, the particular circumstances of each of these three cases may partially explain their higher rates.

The heavy 'combines' were few in number: 41 assessments in 1927 and 65 in 1932. Gross profits were £1.8 m. and £1.4 m. respectively. Figures of average profit, for what they are worth, were £44,000 and £21,000 respectively. This latter figure was still over four times the national average for corporate enterprises, but gross earnings were low in relation to capital charges. These giant enterprises were in fact particularly badly hit by the slump. The figure for Net True Income in 1932 is a mere £150,000.

In the gas industry the setback in total profits was small, from £15.3 m. to £14.6 m., but the fall in numbers was sufficient to yield a higher average profit per unit. This shows a measure of success in adapting itself to the increased competitiveness of electricity, where total and average profits had both risen considerably.

The very large increase in depreciation allowances granted to the retailing trade cannot be explained solely by the increase in numbers. The number of assessments rose by 47,000, or 9 per cent. Wear and tear rose by 89 per cent. Even so, the average allowance per assessment in 1932 was only £12, compared with £7 in 1927. The increase must have been mainly due to the growth of road transport in the distributive trades. No capital allowances were given on buildings in the inter-war period.

[1] Wear and tear allowances were increased by 10 per cent in 1932. This refers to the amount *allowable* rather than to what was actually claimed, but the effect must have been to increase the claims made in 1932 by about £7m., so that only about £4m. or £5m. was in respect of increased capital assets.

The information here is not sufficient to establish a causal relation between profits and capital employed (even so far as this can be indicated by the figures of wear and tear). Did an increase in capital assets provide the means of making large profits? Had past investment decisions accurately predicted the strength of demand? Capital, as measured by wear and tear, increased in 59 trade groups, but in only 20 of them did gross profits increase, and eight of these showed a lower Net True Income. It seems that, while the expansion of capital resources was a necessary condition of profit growth, it was far from being a sufficient condition.

Finally, mention should be made of net profits, although our figures of Net True Income are less reliable than the gross profit figures. The data suggest that, more often than not, increased capital charges did not result in lower net profits for the A groups. Thirteen of them increased their Net True Income, and no substantial decreases occurred in the other eight. On the other hand, all the 57 B groups suffered a fall in Net True Income, including the 18 where depreciation allowances decreased.

One may say in conclusion that both gross and net trading profits tended to show the greatest stability and growth in those trade groups where the wear and tear allowances indicate a significant measure of capital growth, and that the few exceptions to this rule do not disprove it.

III.   1932—1936/8

The last years of our series show the performance of trading profits in a period which covers the last three complete years before the Second War. Apart from the effects of rearmament, which can be seen in the steeply rising profits of heavy industry, the main economic interest of the data lies in plotting the course of the recovery from the depressed conditions of 1932.

For the 78 trade groups which we are considering, total Gross True Income in 1927 was £840 m. This total fell by £176 m. to £664 m. in 1932, then during the next five years rose £370 m. to £1,034 m. During the ten year period from 1927 to 1937, therefore, the net increase in profits was £194 m., or 23 per cent. The following year, 1938, saw a downturn; profits fell by £69 m. to £965 m., which was only 15 per cent above the 1927 level.

If we measure the recovery as the increase from 1932 to 1937, taking our figures of Gross True Income as corresponding very roughly to profits at the bottom and at the peak of the trade cycle, then the compound rate of increase in this period was 9.3 per cent per year. On the other hand, a measure of the secular rate of increase is given very approximately by the rise in profits between 1927 and 1937. This works out at 2.1 per cent per year. Over the longer run therefore the increase in profits appears rather modest; in the shorter period of intensive recovery, the increase appears very rapid.

In contrast to this inter-war period, the 18 years from 'around 1909' to 1927 shows a compound rate of increase of 4.5 per cent per year. However, if we allow for the rise in the general price level between these two years (taking it to be 50 per cent, so that Gross True Income in 1927 was about £555 m. at 1909 prices) then the rate of increase is seen to be 2.2 per cent. The fall in prices between 1927 and 1937 would similarly make the *real* increase in profits between these years rather more than 2.1 per cent per year. This is only a crude calculation, but it does suggest that the increase in profits, measured in real terms, was of the same order between 1909 and 1927 as between 1927 and 1937.

As we shall see in the trade group analysis, the expansion in profits was mainly confined to the corporate organisations. The index numbers of Gross True Income for these in the three pre-war years, with 1927=100, were 135, 151 and 141 respectively. For the non-corporate concerns, the index numbers were 93, 90 and 84. These figures may also be taken as comparable measures of the recovery from 1932, when the index number was 79 for both corporate and non-corporate concerns.

The numbers of enterprises, although varying less than the profit figures, follow the same respective trends. Index numbers for corporate enterprises were 120, 125 and 124; for non-corporate enterprises they were 101, 94 and 93 respectively.

Taking these two series of index numbers together it can be seen that the higher profits of the corporate sector are due partly to their higher relative numbers, and partly to their higher individual profitability. Average profit index numbers are 112, 120 and 114 for the corporate sector, and 93, 95 and 90 for the non-corporate sector.

We have already remarked on the extent of the divergent trends of profit levels after 1927, noting the widening range of movements in industrial and trade group totals during the 1930's. We have also noted the other trend of the numbers of enterprises to remain relatively constant, with a slight downward movement. We now turn to a trade group analysis of the pre-war period, with the main emphasis on those trade groups whose performance was in any way at variance with the general pattern of the time.

(a) *The expanding activities*.

The most spectacular rate of recovery was achieved in the metal trades. With one exception, all these trade groups increased their profit levels significantly more than the average, so that in 1937 and 1938 the totals for the industry were at 240 per cent of the 1927 level. Apart from the distributive sector, it was the largest profit earning 'industry' (in our classification) in the immediate pre-war period. The total profits in 1937 were £149 m., compared with £72 m. earned in Other Manufacturing. As a proportion of the total U.K. profits, the metal industry increased its share from 7.4 per cent in 1927 to 14.4 per cent in 1937 and 15.5 per cent in 1938.

Within the industry, the sector which made the most rapid increase was shipbuilding and heavy engineering, which had been the most severely depressed activities in 1932. The four main trade groups concerned were Iron and steel, Machinery and Engineering, Shipbuilding, and Combines of the above. Their combined profits in the years of our series were respectively £21 m., £35 m., £20 m., £63 m., £87., and £93 m. They were one of the very few large groups which made any noticeable improvement during 1938, a year in which the general level of profits showed a downturn. This was, of course, a period of increasing rearmament.

The total number of enterprises in the metal trades fell by about 10 per cent in the period 1927 to 1938. This fall in numbers was almost wholly confined to the firms and partnerships—each year showed a contraction for most of them, and by 1938 they were two-thirds of their 1927 numbers. The number of corporate assessments was 10 per cent less in 1932, but 20 per cent more in 1936, and 30 per cent more than the 1927 number in the next two years. With one uncertain exception,[1] this proliferation was common to all trade groups in the industry.

The changed organisational structure of this industry is brought out by the following comparison. In 1927, 37 per cent of the concerns were corporate and took 86 per cent of the profits. In 1938, 54 per cent were corporate and took 96 per cent of the profits.

The extractive industry had the second highest rate of increase in profits, but this was due mainly to the recovery in coal mining. Profits

[1] Railway Carriage and Wagon.

from coal mining were between £12 m. and £13 m. in 1927 and 1932, but by 1938 they were almost doubled. Nevertheless, coal had become a less important source of profit than before the First War. In 1909 it accounted for 4.6 per cent of all profits; by 1938 it was only 2.4 per cent.

In contrast to the rise in profits, the number of coal mining concerns fell sharply after 1927, both in the corporate and the non-corporate sectors. Corporate units fell by a third, while their total profits doubled. Non-corporate units fell by a half, but their profits fell correspondingly.

The conversion of coal into power, in the form of electricity and gas, continued to provide a high level of profits. Gas profits did in fact fall slightly, from £14.6 m. in 1932 to £13.5 m. in 1937, but for corporate concerns the average profit increased by about 15 per cent in these five years. In electricity undertakings, profits rose from £26 m. to £32 m. and the average profit also increased considerably.

In the three public utilities, the organisation was almost wholly corporate. The proportion of companies and corporations in the total number of concerns was 85 per cent or over in each year of our series. Their proportion of total profits was never less than 99.7 per cent. In all these activities, including water supply, there was a substantial fall in numbers during the pre-war decade, reflecting the trend towards concentration.

Elsewhere in the economy, the activities to profit most from the expansion in activity follow no particular industrial pattern. In each (so-called) industry except Textiles there were some trades prospering and others declining. As we have noticed before, the expansion was confined mainly to the corporate sector of the economy. Firms and partnerships increased their total profits over the early 1930's, but this rise out of the slump was insufficient to regain the level of 1927. The 1936 profits were still 7 per cent down on 1927, and 1937 and 1938 both saw a decline. The only major trade group in which non-corporate concerns prospered was Road Transport. Profits rose from £10 m. in 1927 to nearly £14 m. in 1936. But again, 1937 and 1938 showed a falling off to £12 m. Even retail distribution, in which over half the total of firms and partnerships were to be found, proved to be a declining source of profit.

Trade groups engaged in the manufacture of consumer durables are included amongst the Metal trades and Other Manufacturing trades, and they will also of course be engaged in producing investment goods. The manufacture of domestic electrical appliances, statistically less important then than now, is not shown separately. It is difficult therefore to gauge the extent of the recovery in consumer manufactures. Judging by the figure given for the various trades in Other Manufacturing, however, it does not appear that this type of activity showed a very pronounced upturn, taking 1927 as a year of comparison. The newer, light engineering products will be included under the Metal trades, but here it is impossible to distinguish between final and intermediate production, and to estimate the amount due to rearmament.

The same sort of difficulty applies to the building trades, where profits showed a fair recovery during the 1930's. It is interesting to note however that despite the boom in housebuilding the Furniture trade group never came very close to the figure of £3.2 m. for profits in 1927, and that the profits in 1937 were lower than in 1936.

The food, drink and tobacco trades as a whole kept very much in step with the general movement in profit levels, although the individual trade groups showed quite a wide range of profit movements. The profits of the nine trade groups as a whole were between 7 per cent and 8 per cent of the total U.K. profits in each year of the series, including 1909. The trade group with the largest increase was Miscellaneous Foods, where profits rose from £7.5 m. in 1927 and in 1932 to £17 m. in 1936 (£14.5 m. in 1937). This is a clear example of a change in consumer demand, showing an increased consumption of modern food preparations.

Profits from brewing and distilling showed very little change between 1927 and 1937, the combined totals being about £30 m. and £31 m. respectively. Tobacco profits in these ten years rose from £12 m. to £15 m.

Transport profits again showed great variation as between trade groups. In 1909, this industry accounted for 20 per cent of total U.K. profits. The growth of cheap transport and the decline of the railways since then are doubtless two of the many causes that brought this proportion down to 11 per cent in 1927, at which level it seemed to remain throughout the 1930's. Road transport continued to expand greatly, profits rising from £25 m. in 1932 to £40 m. in 1937, while the number of enterprises remained approximately the same. Shipping profits were high in this year, at £38 m. but fell by £7 m. the next year. Railways in 1937, at £30 m., had earned only £6 m. more than in the depressed year of 1932.

The one sign of constancy in a changing world was in the field of professional services. Profits fell little, if at all in 1932, and in the last three years, 1936 to 1938, there was very little of the wide annual variation that is found in trade groups in the other industries; 8 or 9 per cent of total profits was a proportion maintained more or less throughout. Obviously, too, most of the 100,000 assessments refer to firms and partnerships. In 1937, only 1.5 per cent were companies, and they earned only 2.4 per cent of total professional profits.

(b) *The contracting activities.*

In discussing those trade groups where profits did not recover their 1927 level during the pre-war period, we shall use the same method as in Section II, distinguishing between A groups and B groups. We are interested here in the B groups, which are defined as those trade groups in which the 1937 Gross True Income was less than in 1927. There were 23 such trades. Their performance is compared with that of the remaining 55 A groups, whose profits did not fall in this period.

1937 is taken in preference to either 1936 or 1938 as a year for comparison. 1937 was a peak year for profits, which were £61 m. higher than the year before and £69 m. higher than the year after. Profit figures should therefore show the best that could be achieved in a good year. It did not of course work out this way in practice for all trades. In some cases, good profits were earned in 1936, with a substantial falling off in the following year. But this going against the tide, as it were, may be taken in some measure as a sign of failure to keep pace with the rest of the economy. There is a possible qualification to this. A low profit level one year, after a good year, may be due to a time lag in the returns from capital formation and re-organisation carried out as a result of the high profits in the period preceding. There is no way of verifying this from the figures given here. There were six trade groups where 1937 profits were lower and 1936 profits higher than in 1927.[1] There were only two trade groups where 1937 profits were lower and 1938 profits higher than in 1937.[2] In fact the general tendency was for the B groups to fall even more in 1938.

Table 6, constructed in the same way as Table 3 in Section II, shows the 23 trade groups in which profits had fallen over the ten year period 1927 to 1937. Seven of these were in the textile trades, four in the food and drink trades, and six in other manufacturing activities.

[1] Wool, Misc. Textiles, Sugar and Glucose, Cocoa and Confectionery, Leather and Rubber, Publishing and Newspapers.
[2] Cocoa and Confectionery, Ships' managers.

The one clear case of a general industrial decline is in textiles. All the non-corporate groups had lower profit totals, and although some of the corporate groups increased a little, the increase was insignificant. Hosiery alone had a degree of success. The diminishing importance of textile production has been noted already. It was felt in both the corporate and non-corporate sectors, although more so in the latter case. By 1938, about 60 per cent of the enterprises were corporate, and these took 90 per cent of the industry's profits.

The textile industry was in fact more corporate than most in terms of numbers. Only public utilities and chemicals had a higher proportion of companies and corporations in their total numbers. But whereas in other industries this feature tended to be associated with high profits, in textiles it was not so, and the heavy falls in profit of the firms and partnerships more than offset the few small increases of the others.

Of the three food trades in our B groups, only Biscuit and Bread declined seriously in the pre-war period. Profits there were at about two-thirds of their 1927 level. These figures, however, refer only to factory production; the baker-retailers are included in the semi-industrial retail trade group. The other two trades, Sugar and Glucose and Cocoa and Confectionery, maintained their profits over the three years very close to the 1927 figure. With the exploitation of new food products during the inter-war period, and the changing of traditional patterns of consumption, it should not be surprising to find opposing trends as between the various trade groups. A more detailed classification of the food trades might illustrate this feature more clearly than the limited figures given here can do.

Of the six B groups included in Other Manufacturing trades, three were connected with clothing of some sort. (In the case of Leather and Rubber, the connection was perhaps only a partial one). Boots and Shoes, and Miscellaneous Clothing in particular showed signs of contraction in both profits and numbers. The latter's profits fell from £10.4 m. in 1927 to £8.5 m. in 1937 and £6.5 m. in 1938. The number of concerns fell by about a quarter.

Taking all the B groups together, and comparing them with the A groups, as is done in part II of Table 6, some interesting differences appear.

As noted already, the fall in profits was more pronounced among the firms and partnerships than the corporate concerns. Fifty trade groups had lower non-corporate profit totals, and only 25 had higher

I. *Analysis of the twenty-three 'B' trade groups, whose Gross True Income in 1937 was less than in 1927.*
II. *Comparison with the fifty-five 'A' trade groups, whose Gross True Income in 1937 was not less than in 1927.*

I The B groups	1937 G.T.I. £mn	Per cent decrease on 1927	Gross True Income		Average Gross True Income		Number of Assessments			Wear & Tear	Net true Income
			C	N.C.	C	N.C.	All	C	N.C.	All	All
Mineral Waters	1.1	42	b	b			b	b	b	b	b
Bleaching and Dyeing	2.4	39	b	b			b	b	b		b
Boots and Shoes	2.6	34	b	b			b	b	b		b
Silk	3.9	31	b	b	b	b	b		b		b
Biscuit and Bread	2.4	30	b	b	b	b	b		b		b
Furniture	2.3	27	b	b	b	b	b		b		b
Lace	.4	24	b	b	b	b	b		b		b
Hotels and Inns	23.1	22	b	b	b	b	b	b	b		b
Soap and Candles	4.4	21	b	b	b	b	b	b	b	b	b
Railways	29.8	20	b	b	b	b	b	b	b		b
Cotton	9.6	19	:	:	:	:	b		:		b
Misc. Clothing	8.5	18	b	b	b	b	b	b	b		b
Ships' managers	.8	14	b	b	b	b	b	b	b		b
Instruments	4.8	13	b	b	b	b	b		b		b
Wool	7.8	12	b	b	b	b	b	b	b	b	b
Gas	13.5	12	b	b	b	b	b		b		b
Leather and Rubber	7.5	12	b	b	b	b	b	b	b		b
Retail (semi-industrial)	78.8	9	b	b	b	b	b		b		b
Cocoa and Confectionery	3.4	8	b	b	b	b	b	b	b		b
Publishing and Newspapers	13.0	6	b	b	b	b	b	b	b		b
Sugar and Glucose	3.5	4	b	b	b	b					b
Flax, Jute, Hemp	2.2	4	b	b	b	b	b	b	b		b
Misc. Textiles	1.0	1	b	b	b	b	b		b		b

II			C	N.C.	C	N.C.	All	C	N.C.	All	All
All B groups	b:		16	20	16	14	18	11	20	3	23
	a:		7	2	7	8	5	12	2	20	—
All A groups	b:		1	30	6	17	34	10	46	—	5
	a:		54	23	49	36	21	45	7	55	50

NOTES. C=corporate enterprises. N.C.=non-corporate enterprises.

The letter 'b' in a column denotes a decrease (of more than 0.5 per cent) in the quantity signified at the head of that column. The letter 'a' denotes an increase, or no change, in the quantity. In part I, the 'a' cells have been left blank.

Owing to the virtual exclusion of Telephones, Railways and Combines of engineering, etc. from the non-corporate sector, this contains only 22 B groups and 53 A groups.

profits. But of these 25, only two were in the B groups. In other words, what brought the B groups down to below their 1927 level was mainly the drastic shrinking of the profits of the non-corporate enterprises. For all the B groups combined the net fall in non-corporate profits was £28 m. in these ten years, compared with a net fall of £13 m. in corporate profits. (These figures are 'net' in that they include the increases which occurred). For all the A groups combined, the net fall of the non-corporate profits was £12 m., against an increase of £246 m. in corporate profits.

In terms of numbers also there was a general contraction in the non-corporate sector, and there is no obvious difference in this respect between the A and B groups. The number of corporate enterprises increased in total, and 57 out of the 78 trade groups increased individually. But a far lower proportion of the B groups increased their corporate numbers, in fact only 12 of the 23, as opposed to 45 of the 55 A groups.

Table 6 shows the effect of this on average profits, so far as they can be estimated. On the whole it seems that the decrease in the corporate enterprises of the B groups led to only a few increases in their average profit, while in the A groups most corporate trade groups had a higher average profit despite their increases in numbers. In other words, establishments seemed to multiply faster where profits were rising than they contracted where profits were falling.

Allowances granted against wear and tear more than doubled in total during these ten years. From a total of £70 m. in 1927, they rose to £131 m. £155 m. and £162 m. respectively in the last three years. These figures, however, give a very imperfect indication of the extent of capital formation, since they also reflect changes in the statutory allowances. The three pre-war years are not comparable with 1927, and the 1938 figure is itself higher than 1937 due partly to increased allowances made in that year.[1]

Only three trade groups had lower wear and tear allowances in 1937 than in 1927, but their combined decrease was only about £100,000. In fact there was practically no decline anywhere, but the A groups accounted for more of the increase than the B groups. The B groups increased their allowances by £11 m., of which nearly £4 m. was accounted for by the semi-industrial retail trades. The A groups increased theirs by £74 m. Some very large increases occurred in coal mining, some of the metal trades, electricity, shipping and road transport.

[1] See Chapter I, p. 12.

The effect of all this on the figures for Net True Income is to make virtually no change in the distinction between the A and B groups. All the B groups had a lower Net True Income, as well as Gross True Income, than ten years earlier. All but five of the A groups had a higher Net True Income, the exceptions being Other Mines, Hosiery, Brewing, Printing and Pottery. This means that despite larger sums for depreciation being deducted from the gross profits of the A groups, their net profits still increased, while the smaller amounts of depreciation deducted from the gross profits of the B groups still left their net profits smaller than ten years before.

In concluding this section on the pre-war period, two points may be made by way of summary. First, although 1937 was in general a successful year for profits, with the highest total figure ever obtained in any year before the Second War, many activities failed to achieve the level of profits obtained in 1927. The Gross True Income in 1927 of the twenty-three B groups in Table 6 represented 32 per cent of the total Gross True Income in that year. In other words, about a third of all profits was earned by trade groups which, ten years later, had not fully recovered from the slump. No doubt individual enterprises in these activities prospered, but they would be exceptions. In 1937, these B groups accounted for only 22 per cent of total profits.

Second, as was noted in Chapter III, the recovery which did occur was confined mainly to the corporate enterprises. Even amongst the A groups in 1937, non-corporate profits were lower than ten years before. Only 33 per cent of total Gross True Income in 1937 was earned by firms and partnerships, compared with 45 per cent in 1927 and 1932. The number of firms and partnerships, as a proportion of the number of all enterprises, appears to have fallen very little, and was still around 90 per cent.

Chapter V

CONCERNS OPERATING OUTSIDE THE UNITED KINGDOM

In the Board's Annual Report, the total income 'arising abroad and accruing to British residents', in so far as it is subject to British income tax, is divided into three Groups.[1] Group I consists of Dominion and Foreign interest and dividends paid through banks and paying agents in this country. Group II consists of (i) the profits of businesses mainly operating abroad, and (ii) investment and other income arising abroad and not included in Group I. Group III consists of the 'foreign' income of concerns which have their main business in the United Kingdom but trade abroad through branches in other countries.

The amount of 'Group III' income is not known, because the income derived by the concerns in question from their overseas branches is not separately assessed to income tax. In the classification used in this report, the 'foreign' income of these concerns is allocated to the trade groups representing the concerns' principal activities, and so tends to inflate the True Income apparently arising from productive activity inside the united Kingdom. The trade groups mainly affected are shipping, banking and insurance, but many trade groups among the manufacturing industries are affected to some extent. If the overseas activities of any concern are in fact carried on by a legally separate company, the True Income from those activities *is* identifiable, and will have been treated as accruing to a 'concern mainly operating abroad'. These concerns are those, like British-owned railway companies and British-owned plantations and mines situated in foreign countries, whose principal fixed assets are situated abroad but which are registered in the United Kingdom. Concerns like shipping companies and export-import concerns are however not treated as 'mainly operating abroad' in spite of the fact that many of their operations are in one sense carried on outside the United Kingdom.

The True Income, representing the trading profits as defined for income tax purposes, of these British concerns operating abroad has been allocated among nine trade groups. The results are shown in the tables presented in this chapter. The classification of the income of

[1] See e.g. 92nd Annual Report, p. 90.

these concerns is necessarily somewhat imprecise, as a result of the impossibility of separating the activities of individual concerns.

In this chapter, as in the rest of this report, the figures for 1909 (1911–12) are estimated and indicate no more than the order of magnitude of the sums concerned. The same convention is also adopted of relating the assessments made in or for a financial period to the appropriate calendar year.

The total amounts of Gross True Income from productive activity abroad, assessed under Schedule D, and the numbers of assessments made in the six years covered by this report, are shown in Table 1. Comparable figures are shown relating to concerns situated in the U.K.

TABLE V.1
Gross True Income and Number of Assessments
British concerns operating abroad compared with those in the United Kingdom[1]

	1909	1927	1932	1936	1937	1938
Gross True Income						
in £ m. (i) Abroad	63	107	49	88	110	93
(ii) In U.K.	370	840	664	973	1.034	965
(iii) Total ..	433	947	712	1,061	1,144	1,058
(i) as per cent of (iii)	14.6	11.3	6.8	8.3	9.6	8.8
Index numbers of G.T.I.						
(1927=100) (i) Abroad ..	59	100	45	82	103	87
(ii) In U.K. ..	44	100	79	116	123	115
Number of Assessments						
in 000's (i) Abroad	3.2	3.5	2.6	2.8	2.8	2.5
(ii) In U.K.	400	1,029	1,077	1,056	993	977
Index numbers of No. of Assts.						
(1927=100) (i) Abroad ..	91	100	73	80	79	73
(ii) In U.K. ..	39	100	105	103	96	95

[1] Assessed *in* 1911–12 (1909) to 1933–34 (1932); assessed *for* 1937–38 (1936) to 1939–40 (1938). All figures exclude interest; U.K. figures exclude profits of agriculture and finance.

The most striking feature of Table 1, is the high, but declining proportion of Gross True Income which was earned by British enterprises abroad during the six years of our series.[1] The proportion in 1909 was as high as 14½ per cent. By 1927, profits arising abroad had increased by about 70 per cent, but U.K. profits had more than doubled, so that the proportion fell. In the slump year of 1932, profits abroad had more than halved since 1927, compared with a fall of one-fifth at home. During the last three pre-war years, profits from abroad had

[1] The proportions, as shown in Table 1, will slightly overstate the actual ratios, since the U.K. figures exclude agriculture and finance, which are included in the overseas figures. The relative fall in overseas profits is still very marked.

recovered fairly well, but the total of £110 m. was only just higher than the 1927 total, and the proportion of these to the overall total had fallen below 10 per cent.

The numbers of assessments shown in Table 1, although an imperfect indicator of the number of enterprises operating in a given year, suggest a downward trend during the inter-war period. Even in the earlier period, from 1909 to 1927, there was a barely significant increase.

Another distinctive feature of the series is the very low proportion of total numbers which were situated abroad, when compared with the corresponding proportion for Gross True Income. Thus in 1937, nearly 10 per cent of total profits were earned by the 0.3 per cent of concerns overseas. It follows of course that the average income of these concerns was considerably higher than that of the U.K. enterprises. This is not surprising, as many of the concerns were heavily capitalized companies operating railways, mineral properties and oil concessions. Another factor is that these concerns, to be included in this group, must have both a head office establishment here as well as an operating establishment abroad. A fairly large minimum size is therefore pre-supposed. The average Gross True Income per assessment of all corporate concerns operating abroad was over £51,000 in 1937, compared with £6,700 for corporate concerns in the U.K.

The other part of Group II income consists of interest and dividends payable abroad, not included in Group I, and income from other foreign possessions, in which profits from productive activity, if included, cannot be distinguished. Most of this composite item therefore consists of non-trading income, with which we are not concerned in this enquiry. Nor does it represent a total of non-trading income earned abroad, since the larger part of this is included in Group I. For the sake of completeness, however, and without further discussion, figures for this item are shown below, together with the totals of Group I income (overseas interest and dividends paid in this country).

IDENTIFIABLE NON-TRADING INCOME FROM ABROAD

			Group II (remainder)	Group I[1]	(£ million)
1909	..	..	8	..	
1927	..	..	37	103	
1932	..	..	28	95	
1936	..	..	27	99	
1937	..	..	28	91	
1938	..	..	27	90	

[1] Source: Inland Revenue reports.

The estimate of £8 m. for 1909 is not comparable with the figures for later years. Before 1914, the income from securities, stocks, shares and rents was chargeable to income tax only if remitted to the United Kingdom. After that date, all such income was chargeable, whether remitted to the U.K. or not.

The relative importance of the various types of British productive activity abroad is shown by the figures of Gross True Income in Table 2, which distinguishes the nine classified trade groups.

TABLE V.2
Gross True Income of concerns operating abroad[1]
£ thousand

	1909	1927	1932	1936	1937	1938
Railways and Transport ..	22,200 ⎫	30,630	9,780	9,730	11,670	9,530
Cables, Telegraphs	⎬	4,710	1,170	1,830	1,770	1,470
Mineral Properties	19,300 ⎫	10,890	6,250	18,130	23,490	20,500
Oil Concessions	⎬	12,670	11,000	15,480	22,450	17.350
Public Utilities	[2]	1,540	1,410	880	1,060	,760
Land and Mortgage Concerns	[2]	1,920	1,030	1,280	1,250	1,080
Plantations	6,850	21,360	2,130	12,360	17,570	11,640
Banks	4,100	4,480	1,590	4,270	3,690	2,950
Other concerns ..	10,500[2]	19,100	14,210	24,210	27,110	27,650
Total	62,950	107,300	48,560	88,170	110,050	92,920

[1] See footnote to Table 1.
[2] Figures for Public Utilities and Land, etc., in 1909 are included in Other Concerns.

Figures for the Gross True Income of each of the nine trade groups in 1909 are not available. It is therefore difficult to break down the increase of £44 m. which had occurred by 1927. Figures for the 'gross assessment' (prior to the various deductions which lead to Gross True Income) can be used to give the orders of magnitude of changes in trading profits. In round figures, then, transport profits increased from £20 m. in 1909 to £30 m. in 1927. In the field of communications the 1927 level of £4.7 m. was roughly double the 1909 figure.

Profits from mineral properties fell sharply during this period. The 1909 figure was between £16 m. and £17 m. In 1927 it was under £11 m. Oil concessions, on the other hand, showed a return which increased over four-fold, from £3 m. to over £12 m.

A large increase, both absolute and proportional, occurred in the Gross True Income arising from plantations. Recorded profits rose from under £7 m. to over £21 m.

The gross assessments for public utilities suggest a slight fall in profits (perhaps £200,000); profits of land and mortgage concerns

G

probably remained about the same. These two trade groups anyway accounted for only a small part of total profits earned abroad. Banking profits, at just over £4 m., rose very slightly, but these too were a small part of the total.

The main increases, therefore, between the pre-War I and post-War I years of our series, occurred in the fields of transport, oil and plantations; the one major decline was in mineral properties. The miscellaneous group showed an increase from about £6 m. to £19 m.

The depressed year of 1932 showed many changes, with an overall decline of nearly £60 m. from the 1927 level. Transport profits fell by £20 m. to one third of their 1927 level. Plantation profits also fell by nearly £20 m. to about 10 per cent of the 1927 figure. Each trade group showed substantial falls, except oil, where the decline was relatively small.

The figures of Gross True Income during the three pre-War II years show the varying degrees of recovery in the eight major trade groups. Profits in transport undertakings remained comparatively low at around £10 m. 1938 in fact produced a worse result that 1932. Three of the smaller trade groups also remained just above or just below the shrunken profit level of 1932. These were cables and telegraphs, public utilities, and land and mortgage concerns.

Between 1927 and 1937 there was however a net increase in the profits of all concerns operating abroad of about £3 m. Over these ten years, mineral properties showed a rise of over £12 m., oil profits rose £10 m., and the miscellaneous concerns had an increase of £8 m.

The other major trade group, plantations, made up a lot of the ground lost during the depression, but the average annual Gross True

TABLE V.3

Percentage shares in Gross True Income earned by British concerns operating abroad.[1]

	1909	1927	1932	1937
Railways, Transport	35⎤	29	20	11
Cables, Telegraphs	⎟	4	2	2
Mineral Properties	31⎟	10	13	21
Oil Concessions	⎦	12	23	20
Public Utilities	—	1	3	1
Land and Mortgage Concerns	—	2	2	1
Plantations	11	20	4	16
Banks	7	4	3	3
Other Concerns	—	18	29	25
Total	—	100	100	100

[1] See footnote to Table 1.

Income for the three years combined was still under £14 m., compared with the £21 m. of 1927. The number of assessments made was only slightly smaller, so that the decline in importance of this activity must be put down to a lower level of profitability, no doubt reflecting falls in the prices of primary products and raw materials.

These changes in relative prosperity and depression of the activities carried on overseas are clearly shown in Table 3, which gives the Gross True Income of each trade group expressed as a percentage of the total income earned by concerns abroad.

One can see here the decline in transport and communications, and in banking, the rise of minerals, oil and miscelleneous concerns, and the severe fluctuations experienced by plantations.

Practically the whole of the Gross True Income recorded for enterprises operating abroad during the inter-war period accrued to corporate concerns (i.e. in effect to public and private companies). Gross True Income for individuals and partnerships never rose as high as £700,000 in any of the five years shown. This is well under one per cent of the total, and was earned mainly by plantations and the miscellaneous group.

A comparison was made at the beginning of this chapter between the performance of concerns operating at home and those operating overseas, in terms of the Gross True Income earned by all enterprises. In view of the virtual exclusion of non-corporate enterprises from most of the overseas activities, a truer comparison would be between the performance of home and overseas corporate enterprises. The appropriate index numbers are as follows:

INDEX NUMBERS OF GROSS TRUE INCOME OF CORPORATE CONCERNS

	1927	1932	1936	1937	1958
Abroad	100	45	83	103	87
In U.K.	100	79	135	151	141

The overall figures for Net True Income and wear and tear allowances for the overseas group are shown in Table 4. Wear and tear, as a proportion of Gross True Income, changed over time to an extent very similar to that in the U.K. 1932, with a W. and T. proportion of 26 per cent for overseas concerns, as against 12 per cent in the U.K., was exceptional, but in that year overseas Gross True Income had fallen more heavily than income at home.

TABLE V.4

Net True Income and Wear and Tear Allowances of all concerns operating mainly abroad[1]

	1909	1927	1932	1936	1937	1938
Wear and tear (£m)	3.7	9.4	12.7	15.0	15.6	15.8
Net True Income (£m) ..	59.3	97.9	35.8	73.1	94.4	77.2
W. and T. as per cent of G.T.I. ..	6	9	26	17	14	17
Above ratio for U.K. concerns ..	6	8	12	13	15	17
Index numbers (1927=100)						
Gross True Income	59	100	45	82	103	87
Net True Income	61	100	37	75	96	79
N.T.I. for U.K. concerns ..	45	100	76	109	114	104

[1] See footnote to Table 1.

The increasing proportion of Gross True Income which was set off against wear and tear is responsible for making the Net True Income series increase at a slower rate than Gross True Income from 1909 to 1927, and decrease at a faster rate thereafter.

For reasons already elaborated,[1] the economic significance of these figures is far from clear. Because of this, the trade group analysis in Table 5 has been confined to three years, 1927, 1932 and 1937. During these years, most of the wear and tear allowances granted to concerns abroad were in respect of transport, mineral, oil and miscellaneous activities. Relative to Gross True Income, large amounts were set off against the profits of the communications group, leaving Net True Income in 1932 and 1937 well under half the level of Gross True Income. One of the largest trade groups, plantations, had relatively very low wear and tear allowances.

TABLE V.5

Net True Income and Wear and Tear of concerns operating mainly abroad[1]
(£ thousand)

	Net True Income			Wear and Tear		
	1927	1932	1937	1927	1932	1937
Railways, Transport	28,000	6,720	9,120	2,630	3,060	2,550
Cables, Telegraphs	3,200	470	650	1,510	700	1,120
Mineral Properties	9,680	4,750	20,650	1,210	1,500	2,840
Oil Concessions	10,700	6,280	17,840	1,970	4,720	4,600
Public Utilities	1,460	1,300	800	80	110	260
Land and Mortgage concerns ..	1,830	1,020	1,230	90	10	20
Plantations	20,980	1,660	16,760	380	470	810
Banks	4,480	1,580	3,670	—	10	20
Other Concerns	17,580	12,060	23,730	1,520	2,150	3,390
Total	97,900	35,820	94,440	9,400	12,740	15,600

[1] See footnote to Table 1.

[1] See Chapter I, page 10.

The number of assessments made on concerns in the various trade groups are shown in Table 6.

TABLE V.6
Number of Assessments on concerns operating abroad[1]

		1909	1927	1932	1936	1937	1938
Railways and Transport	..	410	202	125	117	99	104
Cables, Telegraphs	.. ..	46	80	33	27	27	12
Mineral Properties	.. ..	614	330	264	263	294	231
Oil Concessions	.. ..	69	78	60	57	46	31
Public Utilities	.. ..	67	82	99	62	53	63
Land and Mortgage Concerns	..	194	273	255	156	169	120
Plantations	.. .. ..	930	1,194	486	1,128	1,128	1,018
Banks	.. .. ..	60	35	39	42	20	39
Other Concerns	.. ..	813	1,228	1,192	954	924	925
Total	.. .. ..	3,203	3,502	2,553	2,806	2,760	2,543
of which:							
Corporate ..	.. ..	2,419	2,278	1,520	2,311	2,140	1,888
Non-corporate	.. ..	784	1,224	1,033	495	620	655

[1] See footnote to Table 1.

The largest group numerically was plantations, accounting for 29 per cent of the total assessments in 1909 and 41 per cent in 1937. Apart from the miscellaneous group, the next largest was mineral properties, but the proportion fell from 19 per cent in 1909 to around 10 per cent in the inter-war years. The actual number fell too. The number of assessments on transport concerns also fell heavily, from 400 in 1909 to 100 in the 1930's. This is not necessarily evidence of a decline in the amount of transport equipment still operated by British companies overseas. None of the other trade groups accounted for more than 10 per cent of the total number of assessments in any of the years of the series.

The number of non-corporate enterprises was a very small proportion of the total. Apart from 171 assessments made on non-corporate transport concerns in the assessment year 1911–12, the bulk of these firms and partnerships were engaged in miscellaneous activities, together with between 100 and 200 plantations.

STATISTICAL NOTES TO THE MAIN TABLES

Ideally, the figures shown in these tables would provide measures of the trading profits of specified activities, gross and net of depreciation, and the number of enterprises engaged in these activities, during the six selected calendar years. In fact, the figures provide more or less close estimates of these quantities. The degree of approximation depends partly upon the correspondence between such an ideal set of figures and the quantities which are actually measured. It also depends upon the accuracy with which the statistics produced do in fact measure the quantities they are intended to measure, i.e. certain clearly defined derivatives of the figures of gross assessment. The question of the extent to which they correspond with a hypothetically ideal set of figures is discussed at length in Chapter I, to which reference should be made. These notes are intended solely to describe essential differences in statistical treatment which affect their reliability.

Year of Assessment

Assessments were made *in* the financial years 1911–12, 1928–29 and 1933–34; assessments were made *for* the financial years 1937–38, 1938–39 and 1939–40. Assessments are made, in or for a year, of profits accruing during accounting years which finish within the preceding financial year. Most of the assessments in 1911–12 were based on an average for the three preceding financial years.[1] The period to which assessments refer may be taken, as a convenient approximation, to be the preceding calendar year, i.e. an average of 1908–10 (referred to as '1909'), 1927, 1932, 1936, 1937, and 1938.

Rounding Errors.

Gross and Net True Income. For 1909, estimates existed of the Net True Income of certain trade groups and combinations of trade groups. These were rounded to the nearest £50,000. The figures of Gross True Income for 1909 were obtained by adding the raw figures for Wear and Tear allowances to the N.T.I. estimates. The resulting estimates of G.T.I. are therefore also rounded to £50,000. For the other five years, all G.T.I. and N.T.I. figures are rounded to £10,000.

All totals and sub-totals are separately rounded from the raw figures, so they may not agree with the sums of their constituents. The

---

[1] For details of the exceptions to this rule, see Chapter I, p. 16.

same applies to the separate figures for corporate and non-corporate enterprises, which may not add to the figures for 'all enterprises'.

Wear and Tear Allowances.

These are rounded to £10,000 for all six years.

Number of Assessments.

These are shown precisely.

Average G.T.I. per Assessment.

The averages for *all* enterprises, in Table IX, are rounded to £50. This is not from necessity, but to indicate that these figures have less meaning than those given for corporate and non-corporate concerns separately. The 'profits' of non-corporate enterprises contain a labour and managerial income which is absent from the more purely entrepreneurial income contained in corporate profits. Averaging the two together is therefore confusing two different concepts of income. The averages shown for corporate and non-corporate concerns separately are rounded to £10.

The averages are calculated from the raw figures for G.T.I. Different results may be obtained if the rounded figures of G.T.I. are used. An exception to this is in the case of the 1909 averages, where the rounded G.T.I. figures had to be used.

G.T.I. Index Numbers and Percentage Distribution.

These are also calculated from the raw G.T.I. figures, with the exception again of 1909.

Reliability of the Estimates.

It is not possible to give precise percentage limits within which the 'true' figures may be considered to lie. Apart from the statistical margins of error which could in theory be calculated for the three sample years 1937–38 to 1939–40, other errors will result from the necessity of having to make more or less arbitrary adjustments to many of the individual estimates. These vary from year to year and from trade group to trade group. The considerations to be made in assessing the reliability of the main series of estimates are discussed below.

1909. The figures of Net True Income are taken from an existing set of calculations made by the Inland Revenue. They are partly estimated. Many of the trade groups were combined, and in most cases they have been left in their original combinations in these Main Tables. In some cases, the combinations cut across our breakdown into major branches of activity, and in these cases special estimates have been made. It was assumed for this purpose that the Gross True Incomes of the trade groups within each combination stood in the same ratio to each other as the gross assessments of these trade groups. The existing combinations which were treated in this way were:

{ Shipping and Ships' managers   Adventures O.U.K:
{ Fishing and Trawling

{ Public Utilities
{ Road Transport   { Land and Mortgage Concerns
{ Telephones   { Other Concerns
{ Electricity   { Interest and Other Income

{ Public Amusements
{ Misc. profits n.e.s.
{ Agriculture

The two groups, Agriculture and Interest, etc., from outside the U.K., are excluded for reasons explained in Chapter I. The other combinations had to be split so as to preserve homogeneity in the classifications of Transport, Public Utilities (U.K.), and Miscellaneous Profits.

The Wear and Tear figures for 1909 are not quite comparable with those for later years. In 1909 the taxpayer had to claim the allowance when making his return; after 1923 he could claim it later on the ground of having made an error in his return. The 1909 figures may therefore be somewhat less than they would have been under the later method.

Since the Gross True Income figures for 1909 are obtained by adding the figures for Net True Income and Wear and Tear, there is at least as much uncertainty attaching to them as to the other two sets of figures.

1927 and 1932. The figures for these two years are the most complete, in that full details of most of the adjustments to the gross assessment are available for all trade groups.

1936, 1937 and 1938. The figures for these three years are based on a 20 per cent sample, except that all cases over £1 m. were included. Separate figures for trading losses had to be deducted, and a certain amount of estimation entered into the allocation of these losses among the trade groups for the years 1936 and 1938. For 1937 a full trade-group classification of losses was available. The sums involved are mostly very small, and in any case the losses which are claimed and recorded in any one year relate mainly to losses sustained in previous years. The amount which can be offset against current income will also depend upon the level of income in that year. The interesting quantity would of course be the losses sustained in the current year, but these figures are not available for any of the years covered in this report, and the above treatment conforms to that used for the earlier years.

Order of reliability. In conclusion, one can say that the figures for 1927 and 1932 appear to be more reliable than those for other years, and that the 1909 figures are the least reliable. Also, the overall totals are probably more accurate than the individual trade group figures.

THE MAIN TABLES

A TRADE GROUP ANALYSIS OF SCHEDULE D TRADING AND PROFESSIONAL INCOME, 1909–1938

TABLE I

Gross True Income by Trade Groups
All Enterprises £'000

	1909 (1911–12)	1927 (1928–29)	1932 (1933–34)	1936 (1937–38)	1937 (1938–39)	1938 (1939–40)
Coal Mines	16,950	12,180	12,720	21,240	22,540	23,610
Iron Mines	1,200 ⎱	420	160	220	580	630
Other Mines		750	290	850	860	480
Quarries	1,200	3,410	2,290	4,250	4,930	4,190
EXTRACTION	*19,400*	*16,760*	*15,450*	*26,560*	*28,900*	*28,910*
Cotton	8,600	11,910	3,260	6,610	9,640	6,810
Wool	5,550	8,830	4,920	11,150	7,750	5,060
Silk	⎤	5,680	2,070	4,470	3,930	1,880
Flax, Jute, Hemp		2,290	880	2,150	2,200	1,070
Lace	5,950 ⎬	570	300	490	440	350
Hosiery		3,090	1,970	3,320	3,290	2,840
Misc. Textiles	⎦	1,040	690	1,130	1,030	1,030
Bleaching & Dyeing	2,450	3,990	2,220	1,990	2,410	1,400
TEXTILES	*22,550*	*37,410*	*16,300*	*31,300*	*30,690*	*20,410*
Iron and Steel	⎤	5,160	3,250	12,070	19,040	16,040
Machy. & Engrng.		27,120	15,130	43,110	57,240	61,420
Shipbuilding	20,950 ⎬	1,350	380	2,550	2,890	6,370
Combines of above		1,790	1,380	5,500	8,050	9,350
Rly. Carr. & Wagon	⎩	1,090	650	1,250	1,660	1,800
Motor and Cycle		9,560	5,500	16,740	18,460	17,490
Anchor, Chain, etc.		690	610	2,260	2,560	2,310
Small Arms, Tools, etc.		3,170	2,430	7,060	7,390	8,320
Wrought Iron and Steel Tube	10,150 ⎬	5,680	3,390	9,430	13,640	12,130
Copper and Brass		2,250	1,330	5,010	5,180	4,250
Gold & Silver Plate		1,720	1,130	2,170	1,980	1,840
Lead, Tin, Zinc		1,320	1,680	3,810	5,220	4,550
Tinplate		600	670	2,370	2,330	1,180
Misc. Metals	⎦	640	640	2,460	3,320	2,170
METALS	*31,100*	*62,140*	*38,150*	*115,790*	*148,970*	*149,200*
Grain Milling	⎤	2,660	4,270	5,210	4,780	4,250
Biscuit and Bread (Wholesale)		3,430	2,350	2,000	2,390	2,240
Sugar and Glucose	7,650[1] ⎬	3,670	1,920	3,800	3,520	3,070
Cocoa, Confectionery		3,750	3,470	4,080	3,430	4,030
Misc. Foods	⎦	7,490	7,460	16,890	14,480	12,450
Brewing		24,780	18,850	25,150	25,090	26,050
Distilling	16,850[1] ⎬	5,100	3,370	5,480	5,710	5,810
Mineral Waters, etc.		1,920	1,160	1,620	1,110	1,240
Tobacco	2,800	12,240	10,190	14,180	15,360	15,340
FOOD, DRINK AND TOBACCO	*27,300*	*65,030*	*53,040*	*78,400*	*75,860*	*74,480*
Fine Chemicals	⎤	8,310	9,100	14,390	16,650	13,570
Patent Medicines		1,010	790	1,420	1,460	970
Soap and Candles	9,000 ⎬	5,560	4,010	4,430	4,370	5,250
Fertilisers, Explosives, etc.	⎦	9,580	9,860	13,880	15,000	13,570
CHEMICALS	*9,000*	*24,460*	*23,760*	*34,110*	*37,480*	*33,360*

	1909 (1911–12)	1927 (1928–29)	1932 (1933–34)	1936 (1937–38)	1937 (1938–39)	1938 (1939–40)
Leather and Rubber		8,500	4,460	9,110	7,510	6,840
Boots and Shoes	7,700	3,900	2,260	3,220	2,580	2,200
Misc. Clothing		10,380	5,790	6,700	8,470	6,550
Paper-making		3,960	5,500	8,580	9,060	8,780
Printing, Bookbinding	9,750	7,530	5,480	8,160	7,980	8,080
Publishg., Newspapers		13,900	8,440	14,090	13,020	10,330
Stationery		2,830	2,250	3,770	5,430	4,890
Furniture	2	3,190	1,400	2,560	2,330	1,900
Pottery, China, etc.		1,410	860	1,850	1,400	1,550
Glass	3,800	1,580	1,140	3,790	3,180	3,580
Instruments		5,470	2,680	5,020	4,760	4,910
Manufactures n.e.s.		4,350	4,660	5,450	6,620	4,810
OTHER MANUFCTRG.	21,300²	66,990	44,900	72,290	72,340	64,410
Bldg. & Contracting		16,870	13,260	19,060	19,310	18,810
Bricks, Cement, etc.	9,250²	7,100	5,770	12,110	10,710	11,610
Timber		4,060	3,020	6,900	6,470	4,500
BUILDING	9,250²	28,040	22,050	38,070	36,500	34,920
Gas	8,400	15,340	14,580	13,380	13,460	13,380
Water	6,100	8,690	10,420	11,890	12,140	10,270
Electricity	4,100⁵	16,480	25,520	29,290	31,980	32,320
PUBLIC UTILITIES	18,600	40,520	50,520	54,560	57,590	55,970
MANUFTG. INDUSTRY	139,050	324,570	248,710	424,520	459,440	432,750
Wholesale Distributn.	45,300	84,140	50,580	82,630	87,690	73,710
Hotels, Inns, etc.		29,730	18,100	24,270	23,140	21,410
Retail (purely distributive)	54,300	108,940	95,980	118,520	118,950	109,990
Retail (semi-industrial)		86,700	72,270	84,650	78,780	75,180
DISTRIBUTION	99,650	309,510	236,940	310,070	308,550	280,290
Docks, Canals	4,050	5,490	5,960	5,960	6,530	6,240
Shipping	16,250⁵	23,110	9,300	23,770	38,010	31,020
Ships' managers		950	620	820	820	1,140
Railways	44,800	37,110	23,790	27,380	29,840	27,530
Road Transport	7,000⁵	23,030	24,930	35,800	40,400	38,670
Telephones	1,150⁵	100	270	180	250	180
TRANSPORT	73,250	89,790	64,870	93,910	115,850	104,780
Law		17,130	15,640	18,710	18,970	17,260
Medicine & Dentistry		23,970	24,160	29,280	30,230	29,570
Literature & Art		2,660	2,410	3,410	2,970	2,690
Music and Drama	30,750	2,230	2,260	3,090	3,400	2,980
Accountancy		8,030	8,430	10,930	9,610	9,280
Engrg., Architecture		6,880	5,110	7,970	8,810	8,540
Other Professions		13,750	11,870	15,540	15,320	14,420
PROFESSIONS	30,750	74,650	69,880	88,920	89,310	84,730
Public Amusements	3	7,000	8,660	9,880	12,340	11,010
Fishing & Trawling	850⁵	1,460	950	2,020	1,780	1,420
Markets, Tolls, etc.	1,150	1,630	1,630	1,700	1,640	1,080
Misc. profits, n.e.s.	5,400³'⁵	14,480	16,500	15,580	16,020	20,310
MISCELLANEOUS PROFITS	7,450	24,570	27,740	29,180	31,780	33,820

	1909 (1911–12)	1927 (1928–29)	1932 (1933–34)	1936 (1937–38)	1937 (1938–39)	1938 (1939–40)
U.K. *Total* (excl. Finance)	369,550	839,850	663,600	973,160	1,033,830	965,270
Rlys. & Transport O.U.K.	22,200 ⎫	30,630	9,780	9,730	11,670	9,530
Cables, Telegraphs	⎬	4,710	1,170	1,830	1,770	1,470
Mineral Properties	19,300 ⎫	10,890	6,250	18,130	23,490	20,500
Oil Concessions	⎬	12,670	11,000	15,480	22,450	17,350
Public Utilities	4	1,540	1,410	880	1,060	760
Land, Mortgage Concerns	4	1,920	1,030	1,280	1,250	1,080
Plantations	6,850	21,360	2,130	12,360	17,570	11,640
Banks	4,100	4,480	1,590	4,270	3,690	2,950
Other Concerns	10,500⁴,⁵	19,100	14,210	24,210	27,110	27,650
ADVENTURES O.U.K.	62,950	107,300	48,560	88,170	110,050	92,920
British Banks	⎫	20,020	4,540	−12,550	−14,680	−12,880
Foreign Banks in U.K.	12,800 ⎬	400	450	530	400	250
Insurance	⎭	11,260	12,890	14,790	13,650	13,210
Stockbrokers and Jobbers	9,450	15,540	12,370	15,870	3,550	180
Finance Companies, Bill-brokers	17,250 ⎫	11,820	10,240	12,210	5,480	2,900
Others Brokers & Agents	⎭	8,060	8,230	3,470	8,490	3,330
FINANCE	39,500	67,100	48,720	34,320	16,890	6,990
GRAND TOTAL	472,000	1,014,250	760,880	1,095,650	1,160,770	1,065,180

For 1909:
[1] Sugar and Glucose included in Brewing, etc.
[2] Furniture included in Building.
[3] Public Amusements included in Misc. profits n.e.s.
[4] Public Utilities and Land, etc. included in Other Concerns O.U.K.
[5] Estimated on the basis of the gross *assessment* in 1911–12.

TABLE II
Gross True Income by Trade Groups
Corporate Enterprises £'000

			1927 (1928–29)	1932 (1933–34)	1936 (1937–38)	1937 (1938–39)	1938 (1939–40)
Coal Mines	..	..	11,480	12,260	21,110	22,380	23,290
Iron Mines ..	..	..	400	150	180	480	620
Other Mines	..	..	740	270	810	840	460
Quarries ..	..	..	2,210	1,530	2,720	4,000	3,310
EXTRACTION	..	..	14,830	14,220	24,820	27,690	27,670
Cotton ..	..	..	11,280	3,050	6,370	9,240	6,560
Wool ..	..	..	6,810	3,980	9,880	7,120	4,610
Silk ..	..	..	5,390	1,960	4,360	3,810	1,790
Flax, Jute, Hemp	..	..	1,840	700	1,790	1,910	790
Lace ..	..	..	340	150	340	330	260
Hosiery ..	..	..	2,080	1,560	2,670	2,930	2,080
Misc. Textiles	..	..	810	530	940	880	910
Bleaching and Dyeing	..	..	3,410	1,980	1,580	2,110	1,200
TEXTILES ..	..	..	31,950	13,920	27,920	28,330	18,200

	1927 (1928–29)	1932 (1933–34)	1936 (1937–38)	1937 (1938–39)	1938 (1939–40)
Iron and Steel	4,300	2,800	11,250	17,650	15,500
Machinery and Engineering ..	24,270	13,210	40,720	54,380	59,500
Ship-building	1,100	220	2,180	2,590	6,240
Combines of above ..	1,790	1,380	5,650	8,050	9,450
Rly. Carriage and Wagon ..	1,070	630	1,230	1,630	1,760
Motor and Cycle	8,770	5,030	16,210	17,960	17,000
Anchor, Chain, etc. ..	470	490	1,960	2,330	2,050
Small Arms, Tools, etc.	2,320	1,910	6,330	6,610	7,590
Wrought Iron and Steel Tube	4,970	2,960	8,700	12,880	11,320
Copper and Brass	1,610	1,040	4,630	4,760	3,880
Gold and Silver Plate ..	850	530	1,390	1,350	1,180
Lead, Tin, Zinc	1,240	1,620	3,750	5,170	4,520
Tinplate	470	600	2,270	2,290	1,130
Misc. Metals	370	510	2,240	3,040	1,990
METALS	53,610	32,940	108,540	140,670	143,090
Grain Milling	1,910	3,530	4,160	3,950	3,580
Biscuit and Bread (Wholesale)	3,010	2,140	1,910	2,300	2,150
Sugar and Glucose	3,590	1,850	3,690	3,410	2,970
Cocoa, Confectionery ..	3,420	3,250	3,910	3,290	3,830
Misc. Foods	6,530	6,970	16,270	13,890	12,020
Brewing	23,620	18,400	24,260	24,550	25,620
Distilling	4,990	3,360	5,440	5,660	5,600
Mineral Waters, etc. ..	1,530	890	1,450	890	1,070
Tobacco	12,020	10,040	14,120	15,230	15,270
FOOD, DRINK AND TOBACCO ..	60,600	50,430	75,200	73,160	72,120
Fine Chemicals	7,750	8,720	14,010	16,370	13,340
Patent Medicines	790	660	1,090	1,330	850
Soap and Candles	5,450	3,950	4,390	4,310	5,230
Fertilisers, Explosives, etc. ..	8,650	9,300	12,910	14,290	13,070
CHEMICALS	22,650	22,630	32,400	36,300	32,480
Leather and Rubber ..	6,920	3,650	8,080	6,690	6,160
Boots and Shoes	2,610	1,600	2,610	2,210	1,720
Misc. Clothing	5,600	3,080	3,940	5,950	4,270
Paper-making	3,750	5,340	8,340	8,740	8,360
Printing and Bookbinding ..	4,250	3,090	5,830	5,340	5,550
Publishing and Newspapers ..	12,560	7,720	12,860	11,990	9,720
Stationery	2,150	1,660	2,940	4,870	4,350
Furniture	1,350	490	1,600	1,390	1,180
Pottery, China, etc. ..	1,130	730	1,590	1,240	1,500
Glass	1,340	990	3,650	2,960	3,370
Instruments	4,170	1,860	3,900	3,940	4,070
Manufactures n.e.s. ..	3,280	4,290	5,030	6,260	4,460
OTHER MANUFACTURING ..	49,110	34,500	60,360	61,570	54,730
Building and Contracting ..	5,830	4,820	9,050	9,360	10,090
Bricks, Cement, etc. ..	6,020	5,160	11,410	10,070	11,190
Timber	1,890	1,520	4,470	4,300	3,010
BUILDING	13,750	11,510	24,930	23,720	24,290
Gas	15,320	14,580	13,370	13,450	13,370
Water	8,660	10,390	11,860	12,110	10,240
Electricity	16,420	25,450	29,260	31,920	32,270
PUBLIC UTILITIES	40,400	50,430	54,480	57,480	55,880

	1927 (1928–29)	1932 (1933–34)	1936 (1937–38)	1937 (1938–39)	1938 (1939–40)
MANUFACTURING INDUSTRY ..	272,060	216,340	383,830	421,230	400,790
Wholesale Distribution ..	46,720	29,150	54,330	58,600	47,530
Hotels, Inns, etc.	4,870	2,280	4,600	5,160	4,140
Retail (purely distributive) ..	21,550	24,320	41,540	44,770	39,260
Retail (semi-industrial) ..	8,730	7,390	14,250	13,250	13,120
DISTRIBUTION	81,870	63,140	114,720	121,780	104,040
Docks, Canals	5,420	5,920	5,780	6,480	6,180
Shipping	22,220	8,890	23,130	37,040	30,260
Ships' managers	480	250	430	370	580
Railways	37,130	23,800	27,380	29,840	27,530
Road Transport	12,760	15,040	22,150	27,430	26,510
Telephones	100	270	180	250	180
TRANSPORT	78,100	54,170	79,040	101,400	91,240
Law	10	10	30	—	40
Medicine and Dentistry ..	20	80	50	40	30
Literature and Art	50	30	230	60	40
Music and Drama	10	10	30	30	30
Accountancy	10	20	220	100	20
Engineering and Architecture	210	90	150	330	400
Other Professions	1,020	730	1,290	1,550	1,050
PROFESSIONS	1,320	970	1,990	2,110	1,600
Public Amusements	5,030	7,110	8,180	10,490	9,230
Fishing and Trawling ..	770	570	1,520	1,390	980
Markets, Tolls, etc.	1,400	1,470	1,520	1,380	940
Misc. profits, n.e.s.	5,080	7,250	5,840	6,670	11,820
MISC. PROFITS	12,270	16,400	17,060	19,930	22,960
U.K. Total (excl. Finance) ..	460,460	365,240	621,460	694,140	648,310
Railways and Transport O.U.K.	30,630	9,780	9,730	11,670	9,530
Cables, Telegraphs	4,700	1,170	1,830	1,770	1,470
Mineral Properties	10,890	6,250	18,130	23,490	20,500
Oil Concessions	12,670	11,000	15,480	22,450	17,350
Public Utilities	1,520	1,410	880	1,060	760
Land and Mortgage Concerns	1,840	980	1,280	1,250	1,080
Plantations	20,910	2,030	12,310	17,210	11,530
Banks	4,470	1,590	4,270	3,690	2,950
Other Concerns	18,980	13,940	24,080	26,850	27,250
ADVENTURES O.U.K. ..	106,620	48,150	87,980	109,420	92,420
British Banks	18,460	3,630	−13,380	−15,110	−13,020
Foreign Banks in U.K. ..	400	450	530	400	250
Insurance	9,370	9,490	10,730	10,200	9,310
Stockbrokers, Jobbers ..	50	70	1,080	− 2,300	340
Finance Companies, Bill-brokers	9,430	6,970	11,680	4,730	2,410
Other Brokers and Agents ..	2,650	3,700	− 1,790	3,850	− 2,060
FINANCE	40,350	24,300	8,840	1,780	− 2,770
GRAND TOTAL	607,430	437,690	718,280	805,340	737,950

TABLE III

Gross True Income by Trade Groups.   Non-corporate Enterprises £'000

	1927 (1928–29)	1932 (1933–34)	1936 (1937–38)	1937 (1938–39)	1938 (1939–40)
Coal Mines	690	450	130	160	320
Iron Mines ..	20	10	40	100	20
Other Mines	10	20	50	20	20
Quarries	1,200	750	1,520	940	880
EXTRACTION	*1,930*	*1,230*	*1,740*	*1,210*	*1,240*
Cotton	630	210	250	400	250
Wool	2,020	940	1,260	630	450
Silk	300	100	110	120	80
Flax, Jute, Hemp	460	180	360	290	270
Lace	240	150	150	110	80
Hosiery	1,010	410	650	360	760
Misc. Textiles	230	160	200	150	120
Bleaching and Dyeing	580	240	410	310	200
TEXTILES	*5,460*	*2,380*	*3,380*	*2,370*	*2,220*
Iron and Steel	860	460	820	1,390	550
Machinery and Engineering	2,850	1,910	2,380	2,850	1,920
Shipbuilding	260	160	380	310	130
Combines of above	—	—	−150	—	−100
Rly. Carriage and Wagon	20	20	20	40	40
Motor and Cycle	790	470	530	500	490
Anchor, Chain, etc. ..	220	120	300	230	260
Small Arms, Tools, etc.	850	520	720	790	730
Wrought Iron and Steel Tube	720	420	730	760	810
Copper and Brass	640	280	380	430	370
Gold and Silver Plate	870	590	780	640	650
Lead, Tin, Zinc	80	50	50	50	30
Tinplate	130	70	100	40	50
Misc. Metals	270	130	220	280	190
METALS	*8,540*	*5,210*	*7,250*	*8,300*	*6,100*
Grain Milling	750	730	1,050	830	670
Biscuits and Bread (Wholesale)	430	210	80	100	90
Sugar and Glucose	90	70	110	110	100
Cocoa and Confectionery	320	220	170	140	200
Misc. Foods	960	490	620	590	430
Brewing	1,160	450	900	540	430
Distilling	110	20	40	50	210
Mineral Waters, etc.	390	270	160	220	160
Tobacco	220	150	70	130	70
FOOD, DRINK & TOBACCO	*4,420*	*2,610*	*3,200*	*2,700*	*2,360*
Fine Chemicals	550	370	370	280	230
Patent Medicines	220	130	330	130	120
Soap and Candles	110	70	40	60	30
Fertilizers, Explosives	920	560	970	710	500
CHEMICALS ..	*1,810*	*1,130*	*1,720*	*1,180*	*880*

	1927 (1928–29)	1932 (1933–34)	1936 (1937–38)	1937 (1938–39)	1938 (1939–40)
Leather and Rubber	1,570	810	1,030	820	680
Boots and Shoes	1,290	660	600	380	480
Misc. Clothing	4,780	2,710	2,760	2,520	2,270
Paper-making	210	150	250	320	420
Printing and Bookbinding	3,280	2,390	2,330	2,630	2,520
Publishing and Newspapers	1,350	720	1,230	1,040	600
Stationery	680	590	830	560	540
Furniture	1,830	910	970	940	720
Pottery, China, etc.	270	130	260	160	50
Glass	240	150	150	220	210
Instruments	1,300	820	1,120	830	840
Manufactures n.e.s.	1,070	370	420	360	350
OTHER MANUFACTURING	*17,880*	*10,410*	*11,930*	*10,770*	*9,690*
Building and Contracting	11,040	8,430	10,010	9,950	8,720
Bricks, Cement, etc.	1,080	610	700	650	420
Timber	2,170	1,500	2,430	2,180	1,500
BUILDING	*14,280*	*10,550*	*13,140*	*12,780*	*10,630*
Gas	20	−10	10	20	10
Water	30	30	30	30	30
Electricity	70	70	30	60	50
PUBLIC UTILITIES	*120*	*90*	*80*	*110*	*90*
MANUFACTURING INDUSTRY	*52,510*	*32,370*	*40,690*	*38,210*	*31,960*
Wholesale Distribution	37,420	21,430	28,300	29,080	26,190
Hotels, Inns, etc.	24,860	15,820	19,670	17,980	17,270
Retail (purely distributive)	87,380	71,670	76,980	74,190	70,730
Retail (semi-industrial)	77,970	64,880	70,400	65,520	62,060
DISTRIBUTION	*227,630*	*173,800*	*195,350*	*186,770*	*176,250*
Docks, Canals	70	40	180	50	60
Shipping	890	410	640	970	760
Ships' managers	480	370	380	460	560
Railways	−10	−10	—	—	—
Road Transport	10,260	9,890	13,650	12,970	12,160
Telephones	—	—	—	—	—
TRANSPORT	*11,690*	*10,710*	*14,860*	*14,450*	*13,540*
Law	17,120	15,630	18,680	18,970	17,230
Medicine and Dentistry	23,950	24,080	29,230	30,190	29,540
Literature and Art	2,620	2,380	3,180	2,910	2,650
Music and Drama	2,220	2,250	3,070	3,370	2,950
Accountancy	8,020	8,410	10,710	9,510	9,260
Engineering and Architecture	6,670	5,020	7,820	8,490	8,140
Other Professions	12,730	11,140	14,260	13,770	13,370
PROFESSIONS	*73,330*	*68,910*	*86,940*	*87,200*	*83,130*
Public Amusements	1,970	1,550	1,700	1,850	1,780
Fishing and Trawling	690	380	510	390	440
Markets, Tolls, etc.	230	160	190	260	140
Misc. profits n.e.s.	9,400	9,250	9,740	9,350	8,490
MISC. PROFITS	*12,300*	*11,340*	*12,130*	*11,850*	*10,860*

H

	1927 (1928–29)	1932 (1933–34)	1936 (1937–38)	1937 (1938–39)	1938 (1939–40)
U.K. Total (Excl. Finance) ..	379,390	298,360	351,700	339,690	316,960
Railways and Transport O.U.K.	—	−10	—	—	—
Cables, Telegraphs	—	—	—	—	—
Mineral Properties	—	—	—	—	—
Oil Concessions	—	—	—	—	—
Public Utilities	20	—	—	—	—
Land, Mortgage Concerns ..	80	50	—	—	—
Plantations	450	100	60	360	110
Banks	—	—	—	—	—
Other Concerns	120	270	130	260	400
ADVENTURES O.U.K. ..	690	420	190	620	510
British Banks	1,560	910	830	430	140
Foreign Banks in U.K. ..	—	—	—	—	—
Insurance	1,900	3,400	4,060	3,450	3,900
Stockbrokers and Jobbers ..	15,490	12,300	14,790	5,860	−160
Finance Companies, Bill-brokers	2,390	3,270	530	750	490
Other brokers and Agents ..	5,410	4,530	5,260	4,640	5,390
FINANCE	26,750	24,410	25,480	15,120	9,760
GRAND TOTAL	406,820	323,190	377,370	355,430	327,230

TABLE IV

Wear and Tear Allowances by Trade Groups.   All Enperprises, £'000

	1909[1] (1911–12)	1927 (1928–29)	1932 (1933–34)	1936 1937–38)	1937 (1938–39)	1938 (1939–40)
Coal Mines	740	1,530	3,560	4,630	4,610	4,510
Iron Mines	20	20	30	40	40	30
Other Mines	50	90	80	90	200	40
Quarries	70	350	510	660	1,170	850
EXTRACTION	890	1,990	4,180	5,410	6,030	5,440
Cotton	1,340	2,940	1,130	2,780	4,170	2,570
Wool	650	1,290	1,250	1,940	1,240	1,560
Silk	70	1,530	680	1,800	1,780	1,050
Flax, Jute, Hemp ..	340	340	380	590	440	220
Lace	120	80	80	130	110	60
Hosiery	90	530	660	1,070	1,240	1,130
Misc. Textiles	30	110	100	180	190	150
Bleaching and Dyeing ..	340	610	770	620	700	500
TEXTILES	2,990	7,430	5,060	9,100	9,850	7,250

	1909[1] (1911–12)	1927 (1928–29)	1932 (1933–34)	1936 (1937–38)	1937 (1938–39)	1938 (1939–40)
Iron and Steel	730	830	1,430	2,450	2,950	3,030
Machinery & Engineering	900	2,630	2,410	5,950	7,920	9,160
Shipbuilding	250	270	370	640	660	1,780
Combines of above ..	350	350	1,230	1,270	1,320	1,530
Rly. Carriage and Wagon ..	100	210	330	250	520	240
Motor and Cycle ..	90	830	860	2,520	2,980	4,870
Anchor, Chain, etc. ..	50	130	100	340	460	430
Small Arms, Tools, etc. ..	100	320	290	790	700	980
Wrought Iron & Steel Tube	190	730	720	1,530	2,060	1,600
Copper and Brass	80	180	200	430	560	420
Gold and Silver Plate ..	30	70	70	280	150	180
Lead, Tin, Zinc ..	40	250	230	520	530	670
Tinplate	30	60	250	400	560	200
Misc. Metals	20	80	130	340	400	370
METALS	2,970	6,930	8,610	17,690	21,780	25,450
Grain Milling	230	480	550	690	660	650
Biscuit and Bread (Wholesale)	40	340	410	560	590	740
Sugar and Glucose ..	20	440	310	600	560	290
Cocoa and Confectionery	70	440	550	620	710	800
Misc. Foods	170	1,020	1,050	2,490	2,690	2,490
Brewing	} 400	890	1,010	1,560	1,740	3,010
Distilling		60	60	80	150	110
Mineral Waters, etc. ..		170	180	260	150	240
Tobacco	60	300	380	490	610	580
FOOD, DRINK, TOBACCO ..	990	4,130	4,510	7,350	7,860	8,890
Fine Chemicals	190	940	1,960	4,060	4,830	4,950
Patent Medicines ..	—	10	10	30	40	20
Soap and Candles ..	100	430	410	370	390	640
Fertilizers, Explosives, etc.	210	1,240	1,510	1,670	2,260	1,820
CHEMICALS	510	2,620	3,890	6,120	7,520	7,430
Leather and Rubber ..	130	700	890	1,810	1,460	1,460
Boots and Shoes ..	90	280	240	440	310	210
Misc. Clothing ..	100	540	500	700	860	780
Paper-making	350	810	1,430	2,190	2,310	2,410
Printing, Bookbinding ..	340	970	1,040	1,580	1,800	2,170
Publishing & Newspapers	260	940	1,060	1,310	1,460	1,280
Stationery	60	250	320	580	760	810
Furniture	[2]	110	130	210	230	250
Pottery, China, etc. ..	20	60	60	120	120	190
Glass	10	150	320	490	480	620
Instruments	40	290	270	540	600	830
Manufacturing n.e.s. ..	50	310	730	600	620	710
OTHER MANUFACTURING ..	1,440[2]	5,400	6,990	10,570	10,990	11,710
Building and Contracting	100	620	890	1,450	1,880	1,780
Bricks, Cement, etc. ..	140	900	980	1,470	1,780	2,090
Timber	110[2]	300	310	830	780	540
BUILDING	340[2]	1,820	2,190	3,750	4,440	4,410
Gas	30	1,390	2,090	2,300	2,530	2,780
Water	20	120	590	660	560	570
Electricity	1,160	4,400	8,540	11,640	15,110	15,760
PUBLIC UTILITIES ..	1,210	5,910	11,220	14,590	18,200	19,110

	1909[1] (1911–12)	1927 (1928–29)	1932 (1933–34)	1936 1937–38)	1937 (1938–39)	1938 (1939–40)
MANUFACTURING INDUSTRY	10,450	34,240	42,460	69,180	80,630	84,250
Wholesale Distribution ..	720	4,960	4,820	6,500	8,040	6,730
Hotels, Inns, etc. ..	30	230	280	420	530	430
Retail (purely distributive)	140	2,040	4,040	5,850	7,050	7,640
Retail (semi-industrial) ..	150	1,660	2,940	7,710	5,520	5,520
DISTRIBUTION	1,030	8,890	12,080	20,480	21,140	20,330
Docks, Canals	170	340	470	380	450	440
Shipping	7,480	16,390	10,170	16,770	24,230	20,150
Ships' managers ..	10	60	40	50	90	20
Railways	320	50	670	1,020	1,110	10,800
Road Transport ..	1,820	6,400	9,370	13,610	16,200	16,470
Telephones	—	50	70	50	150	130
TRANSPORT	9,800	23,290	20,790	31,880	42,230	48,010
Law	—	10	20	40	40	50
Medicine and Dentistry ..	—	350	530	730	860	840
Literature and Art	—	10	10	100	40	20
Music and Drama ..	—	10	20	30	30	60
Accountancy	—	10	30	40	50	60
Engineering & Architecture	—	40	60	100	120	130
Other Professions ..	—	100	150	260	300	320
PROFESSIONS ..	—	530	830	1,300	1,440	1,480
Public Amusements ..	40	270	540	800	1,190	1,160
Fishing and Trawling ..	370	650	550	820	820	670
Markets, Tolls, etc. ..	20	30	40	220	30	60
Misc. profits n.e.s. ..	80	320	390	740	1,030	1,020
MISC. PROFITS	510	1,280	1,520	2,580	3,070	2,910
U.K. Total (excl. Finance)	22,680	70,200	81,870	130,820	154,540	162,400
Rlys. & Transport O.U.K.	610	2,630	3,060	2,500	2,550	2,990
Cables, Telegraphs ..	830	1,510	700	1,170	1,120	1,040
Mineral Properties ..	1,390	1,210	1,500	3,400	2,840	3,240
Oil Concessions ..	220	1,970	4,720	3,860	4,600	3,760
Public Utilities	80	80	110	220	260	230
Land & Mortgage Concerns	10	90	10	20	20	20
Plantations	110	380	470	620	810	670
Banks	—	—	10	30	20	30
Other Concerns ..	470	1,520	2,150	3,200	3,390	3,790
ADVENTURES O.U.K. ..	3,720	9,400	12,740	15,020	15,600	15,770
British Banks	—	—	90	80	20	10
Foreign Banks in U.K. ..	—	—	—	—	—	—
Insurance	—	20	60	120	320	180
Stockbrokers & Jobbers	—	—	—	150	30	10
Finance Companies, Bill-brokers	10 ⎱	190	310	170	80	160
Other Brokers and Agents	⎰	90	150	550	330	330
FINANCE	10	300	620	1,060	780	680
GRAND TOTAL	26,410	79,910	95,240	146,900	170,930	178,850

[1] Estimated.   [2] Furniture included in Timber.

TABLE V

Net True Income by Trade Groups. All Enterprises £'000

	1909 (1911–12)	1927 (1928–29)	1932 (1933–34)	1936 (1937–38)	1937 (1938–39)	1938 (1939–40)
Coal Mines	16,200	10,650	9,160	16,610	17,920	19,100
Iron Mines	⎱ 1,150	400	130	180	540	600
Other Mines	⎰	660	210	770	650	430
Quarries	1,150	3,060	1,770	3,590	3,760	3,350
EXTRACTION	*18,500*	*14,770*	*11,270*	*21,150*	*22,870*	*23,480*
Cotton	7,250	8,970	2,130	3,830	5,470	4,240
Wool	4,900	7,540	3,670	9,210	6,510	3,500
Silk		4,150	1,390	2,670	2,150	820
Flax, Jute, Hemp		1,950	500	1,560	1,770	840
Lace	5,300	490	220	360	330	280
Hosiery		2,560	1,310	2,250	2,060	1,710
Misc. Textiles		930	590	960	850	870
Bleaching and Dyeing	2,100	3,380	1,450	1,370	1,720	900
TEXTILES	*19,550*	*29,970*	*11,250*	*22,200*	*20,840*	*13,170*
Iron and Steel		4,330	1,820	9,620	16,090	13,010
Machinery & Engineering	18,700	24,490	12,720	37,160	49,310	52,260
Shipbuilding		1,080	10	1,920	2,240	4,590
Combines of above		1,440	150	4,230	6,730	7,810
Rly. Carriage & Wagon		880	320	1,000	1,140	1,560
Motor and Cycle		8,730	4,640	14,220	15,480	12,620
Anchor, Chain, etc.		560	510	1,930	2,100	1,880
Small Arms, Tools, etc.		2,850	2,140	6,270	6,690	7,340
Wrought Iron & Steel Tube	9,400	4,950	2,670	7,900	11,580	10,530
Copper and Brass		2,070	1,130	4,580	4,620	3,830
Gold and Silver Plate		1,650	1,060	1,890	1,830	1,660
Lead, Tin, Zinc		1,070	1,450	3,290	4,690	3,880
Tinplate		540	420	1,970	1,770	980
Misc. Metals		560	510	2,120	2,930	1,810
METALS	*28,100*	*55,210*	*29,540*	*98,100*	*127,200*	*123,750*
Grain Milling		2,180	3,720	4,520	4,120	3,610
Biscuit & Bread (Wholesale)		3,090	1,940	1,440	1,810	1,500
Sugar and Glucose	7,150[1]	3,230	1,610	3,200	2,960	2,780
Cocoa and Confectionery		3,310	2,920	3,460	2,720	3,240
Misc. Foods		6,470	6,410	14,400	11,780	9,960
Brewing		23,890	17,840	23,590	23,350	23,050
Distilling	16,400[1]	5,040	3,310	5,400	5,560	5,700
Mineral Waters, etc.		1,750	980	1,360	960	1,000
Tobacco	2,750	11,940	9,810	13,690	14,750	14,760
FOOD, DRINK & TOBACCO	*26,300*	*60,900*	*48,530*	*71,050*	*68,000*	*65,580*
Fine Chemicals		7,370	7,140	10,330	11,830	8,620
Patent Medicines	8,500	1,000	780	1,390	1,420	950
Soap and Candles		5,130	3,600	4,060	3,980	4,610
Fertilizers, Explosives, etc.		8,340	8,350	12,210	12,740	11,750
CHEMICALS	*8,500*	*21,840*	*19,870*	*27,990*	*29,960*	*25,940*

	1909 (1911–12)	1927 (1928–29)	1932 (1933–34)	1936 (1937–38)	1937 (1938–39)	1938 (1939–40)
Leather and Rubber ..	⎫	7,800	3,570	7,300	6,050	5,380
Boots and Shoes ..	7,400 ⎬	3,620	2,020	2,770	2,270	2,000
Misc. Clothing ..	⎭	9,840	5,290	6,000	7,610	5,770
Paper-making	⎫	3,150	4,070	6,390	6,760	6,370
Printing, Bookbinding ..	8,750 ⎬	6,560	4,440	6,580	6,180	5,910
Publishing & Newspapers	⎪	12,960	7,380	12,780	11,570	9,040
Stationery	⎭	2,580	1,930	3,190	4,670	4,080
Furniture	2	3,080	1,270	2,360	2,100	1,650
Pottery, China, etc. ..	⎫	1,350	800	1,730	1,280	1,360
Glass	3,700 ⎬	1,430	820	3,300	2,710	2,960
Instruments	⎪	5,180	2,410	4,470	4,160	4,080
Manufactures n.e.s. ..	⎭	4,040	3,930	4,850	6,010	4,100
OTHER MANUFACTURING	19,850²	61,590	37,910	61,720	61,350	52,700
Building & Contracting	⎫	16,250	12,370	17,620	17,430	17,030
Bricks, Cement, etc. ..	8,900² ⎬	6,200	4,790	10,640	8,940	9,510
Timber	⎭	3,760	2,710	6,070	5,690	3,970
BUILDING	8,900²	26,220	19,860	34,320	32,060	30,510
Gas	8,350	13,950	12,490	11,080	10,930	10,610
Water..	6,100	8,570	9,830	11,230	11,590	9,700
Electricity	2,950⁵	12,080	16,980	17,650	16,870	16,560
PUBLIC UTILITIES ..	17,400	34,610	39,290	39,970	39,390	36,860
MANUFACTURG. INDUSTRY	128,600	290,340	206,250	355,340	378,810	348,500
Wholesale Distribution ..	44,600	79,180	45,760	76,130	79,640	66,980
Hotels, Inns, etc.	⎫	29,500	17,820	23,850	22,610	20,980
Retail (purely distributive)	54,000 ⎬	106,900	91,940	112,680	111,900	102,350
Retail (semi-industrial) ..	⎭	85,040	69,330	76,940	73,250	69,660
DISTRIBUTION	98,600	300,620	224,860	289,590	287,410	259,960
Docks, Canals ..	3,900	5,150	5,490	5,580	6,080	5,810
Shipping	8,750⁵ ⎫	6,720	−870	7,010	13,780	10,860
Ships' managers ..	⎭	890	580	760	740	1,120
Railways	44,500	37,060	23,120	26,360	28,720	16,730
Road Transport ..	5,150⁵	16,620	15,560	22,190	24,200	22,200
Telephones	1,150⁵	50	200	130	100	50
TRANSPORT	63,450	66,500	44,080	62,030	73,630	56,770
Law	⎫	17,120	15,620	18,670	18,930	17,210
Medicine and Dentistry	⎪	23,620	23,630	28,550	29,370	28,730
Literature and Art ..	⎪	2,650	2,400	3,310	2,930	2,670
Music and Drama ..	30,750 ⎬	2,220	2,240	3,060	3,360	2,920
Accountancy	⎪	8,020	8,400	10,890	9,560	9,220
Engineering, Architecture	⎪	6,840	5,050	7,870	8,690	8,410
Other Professions ..	⎭	13,650	11,720	15,280	15,020	14,100
PROFESSIONS	30,750	74,120	69,050	87,620	87,870	83,250
Public Amusements ..	3	6,730	8,120	9,070	11,150	9,850
Fishing and Trawling ..	500⁵	810	400	1,200	960	750
Markets, Tolls, etc. ..	1,150	1,600	1,590	1,490	1,610	1,020
Misc. Profits n.e.s. ..	5,300³,⁵	14,160	16,110	14,840	14,990	19,290
MISC. PROFITS	6,950	23,300	26,220	26,610	28,710	30,910
U.K. Total (excl. Finance)	346,850	769,640	581,730	842,340	879,290	802,870

	1909 (1911–12)	1927 (1928–29)	1932 (1933–34)	1936 (1937–38)	1937 (1938–39)	1938 (1939–40)
Rlys. & Transport O.U.K.	20,750 ⎱	28,000	6,720	7,230	9,120	6,550
Cables, Telegraphs ..		3,200	470	670	650	430
Mineral Properties ..	17,700 ⎱	9,680	4,750	14,730	20,650	17,260
Oil Concessions ..	⎰	10,700	6,280	11,610	17,840	13,590
Public Utilities ..	[4]	1,460	1,300	650	800	530
Land, Mortgage Concerns	[4]	1,830	1,020	1,260	1,230	1,060
Plantations	6,750	20,980	1,660	11,750	16,760	10,970
Banks..	4,100	4,480	1,580	4,240	3,670	2,920
Other Concerns ..	9,950[4,5]	17,580	12,060	21,010	23,730	23,860
ADVENTURES O.U.K. ..	59,250	97,900	35,820	73,150	94,440	77,150
British Banks	⎱	20,020	4,450	−12,630	−14,700	−12,890
Foreign Banks in U.K. ..	12,800 ⎬	400	450	530	400	250
Insurance	⎰	11,240	12,830	14,670	13,330	13,030
Stockbrokers and Jobbers	9,450	15,540	12,370	15,720	3,520	170
Finance Companies, Bill-Brokers	17,250 ⎬	11,630	9,930	12,040	5,400	2,750
Other Bankers & Agents	⎰	7,970	8,080	2,920	8,170	2,990
FINANCE	39,500	66,800	48,090	33,260	16,110	6,310
GRAND TOTAL	445,600	934,340	665,640	948,750	989,840	886,330

For 1909:
[1] Sugar and Glucose included in Brewing, etc.
[2] Furniture included in Building.
[3] Public Amusements included in Misc. profits n.e.s.
[4] Public Utilities and Land, etc., included in Other Concerns O.U.K.
[5] Estimated on the basis of the gross *assessment* in 1911–**12.**

TABLE VI

*Number of **Assessments** in Trade Groups. All Enterprises*

	1909 (1911–12)	1927 (1928–29)	1932 (1933–34)	1936 (1937–38)	1937 (1938–39)	1938 (1939–40)
Coal Mines	1,433	1,623	1,238	950	1,010	940
Iron Mines	78	70	50	56	73	56
Other Mines	273	161	141	156	131	112
Quarries	4,131	3,151	2,934	2,422	2,347	2,310
EXTRACTION	5,915	5,005	4,363	3,584	3,561	3,418
Cotton	1,836	1,931	1,154	1,312	1,255	1,117
Wool	1,652	1,910	1,605	1,711	1,543	1,330
Silk	174	471	472	468	505	401
Flax, Jute, Hemp ..	956	1,088	829	1,084	807	909
Lace	633	481	407	422	391	295
Hosiery	318	970	925	835	766	857
Misc. Textiles	406	472	436	486	446	396
Bleaching and Dyeing ..	679	794	635	584	565	528
TEXTILES	6,654	8,117	6,463	6,902	6,278	5,833

	1909 (1911–12)	1927 (1928–29)	1932 (1933–34)	1936 (1937–38)	1937 (1938–39)	1938 (1939–40)
Iron and Steel ..	1,293	1,637	1,320	1,715	1,641	1,675
Machinery & Engineering	3,325	8,088	7,457	8,035	8,205	7,756
Shipbuilding ..	295	794	704	764	783	729
Combines of above ..	20	41	65	82	71	71
Rly. Carriage and Wagon	82	140	112	106	76	116
Motor and Cycle ..	768	2,346	2,079	2,027	1,914	2,032
Anchor, Chain, etc. ..	312	501	375	503	435	409
Small Arms, Tools, etc. ..	1,190	2,660	2,161	2,113	1,888	2,273
Wrought Iron & Steel Tube	1,064	1,923	1,658	2,000	2,100	1,894
Copper and Brass ..	783	1,326	1,064	1,086	1,173	996
Gold and Silver Plate ..	1,242	1,931	1,716	1,613	1,473	1,381
Lead, Tin, Zinc	202	244	252	237	237	226
Tinplate	61	254	220	209	204	199
Misc. Metals	370	629	539	685	597	551
METALS	*11,007*	*22,514*	*19,722*	*21,175*	*20,797*	*20,308*
Grain Milling	1,503	2,044	1,924	1,973	1,583	1,411
Biscuit & Bread (Wholesale)	131	395	439	434	427	525
Sugar and Glucose ..	46	203	186	297	220	235
Cocoa and Confectionery	492	822	805	804	634	708
Misc. Foods	1,108	1,695	1,749	1,806	1,601	1,571
Brewing		1,608	1,402	1,238	1,280	1,271
Distilling	2,921	117	73	98	118	93
Mineral Waters, etc. ..		1,050	804	533	527	491
Tobacco	228	240	270	238	239	218
FOOD, DRINK & TOBACCO	*6,429*	*8,174*	*7,652*	*7,421*	*6,629*	*6,523*
Fine Chemicals ..	790	1,296	1,341	1,464	1,411	1,508
Patent Medicines ..	162	181	185	213	192	165
Soap and Candles ..	203	271	296	185	225	231
Fertilizers, Explosives, etc.	1,500	1,966	1,881	1,858	1,873	1,709
CHEMICALS	*2,655*	*3,714*	*3,703*	*3,720*	*3,701*	*3,613*
Leather and Rubber ..	1,909	2,817	2,291	2,368	2,120	1,963
Boots and Shoes ..	977	2,365	1,928	1,610	1,145	1,140
Misc. Clothing ..	3,490	8,397	7,688	7,082	6,376	5,948
Paper-making ..	303	539	556	598	628	540
Printing and Bookbinding	3,966	7,756	7,585	7,684	6,949	7,049
Publishing & Newspapers	1,511	1,840	1,698	1,944	1,926	1,868
Stationery	718	1,500	1,341	1,570	1,610	1,445
Furniture	[2]	3,298	2,834	2,310	2,107	2,086
Pottery, China, etc. ..	391	563	355	432	502	445
Glass	364	415	384	410	430	445
Instruments	1,457	3,210	3,104	3,013	2,488	3,633
Manufactures n.e.s.	921	1,564	1,407	1,385	1,329	1,259
OTHER MANUFACTURING	*16,007*[2]	*34,264*	*31,171*	*30,406*	*27,610*	*27,821*
Building and Contracting	9,284	16,986	17,427	18,479	17,527	16,286
Bricks, Cement, etc. ..	1,949	2,257	2,119	2,280	2,160	1,946
Timber	4,704[2]	5,427	5,056	5,212	4,353	4,197
BUILDING	*15,937*[2]	*24,670*	*24,602*	*25,971*	*24,040*	*22,429*
Gas	1,626	1,498	1,333	1,125	1,059	1,123
Water..	2,665	2,066	2,060	1,783	1,682	1,586
Electricity	491	1,040	1,053	945	935	810
PUBLIC UTILITIES ..	*4,782*	*4,604*	*4,446*	*3,853*	*3,676*	*3,519*

	1909 (1911–12)	1927 (1928–29)	1932 (1933–34)	1936 (1937–38)	1937 (1938–39)	1938 (1939–40)
MANUFACTURING INDUSTRY	63,471	106,057	97,759	99,448	92,731	90,046
Wholesale Distribution ..	31,160	58,346	54,091	52,571	48,986	47,491
Hotels, Inns, etc. ..	46,253	79,315	76,567	74,186	61,026	59,946
Retail (purely distributive)	82,225	296,956	322,098	315,340	307,686	301,836
Retail (semi-industrial) ..	47,557	244,445	266,126	264,313	249,138	243,198
DISTRIBUTION	207,195	679,062	718,882	706,410	666,836	652,471
Docks, Canals ..	527	484	471	410	360	365
Shipping	3,275	1,913	1,393	1,648	1,624	1,575
Ships' managers ..	654	524	362	331	306	316
Railways	172	112	104	37	33	35
Road Transport ..	4,150	30,164	34,704	35,487	30,007	34,112
Telephones	14	21	31	35	40	41
TRANSPORT	8,792	33,218	37,065	37,948	32,370	36,444
Law	13,314	12,706	12,495	12,625	12,385	12,420
Medicine and Dentistry	22,278	30,930	32,219	31,795	31,117	30,770
Literature and Art ..	5,256	7,726	8,735	8,690	8,225	8,040
Music and Drama ..	4,490	7,789	9,208	9,110	8,781	7,855
Accountancy	3,448	7,833	8,520	9,634	9,189	9,674
Engineering, Architecture	6,685	8,481	8,173	8,395	8,120	7,870
Other Professions ..	19,981	31,379	35,442	34,615	32,130	31,900
PROFESSIONS	75,452	106,844	114,792	114,864	109,947	108,529
Public Amusements ..	2,811	8,620	8,555	7,859	7,945	7,870
Fishing and Trawling ..	1,783	3,232	2,603	2,585	1,922	1,898
Markets, Tolls, etc. ..	4,502	4,777	3,615	2,755	2,295	2,005
Misc. profits n.e.s. ..	29,604	81,935	88,909	80,734	75,020	74,800
MISC. PROFITS	38,700	98,564	103,682	93,933	87,182	86,573
U.K. Total (excl. Finance)	399,525	1,028,750	1,076,543	1,056,187	992,627	977,481
Rlys. and Transport O.U.K.	410	202	125	117	99	104
Cables, Telegraphs ..	46	80	33	27	27	12
Mineral Properties ..	614	330	264	263	294	231
Oil Concessions ..	69	78	60	57	46	31
Public Utilities ..	67	82	99	62	53	63
Land & Mortgage Concerns	194	273	255	156	169	120
Plantations	930	1,194	486	1,128	1,128	1,018
Banks..	60	35	39	42	20	39
Other Concerns ..	813	1,228	1,192	954	924	925
ADVENTURES O.U.K. ..	3,203	3,502	2,553	2,806	2,760	2,543
British Banks	181 }	165	155	160	162	142
Foreign Banks in U.K. ..		31	32	31	24	24
Insurance	1,174	5,869	6,744	5,951	5,632	5,892
Stockbrokers and Jobbers	3,410	2,827	2,574	2,558	1,941	1,951
Finance Companies, Bill-brokers	3,785	4,312	3,719	3,913	3,466	3,237
Other Brokers & Agents	11,191	12,872	13,158	12,034	10,274	10,553
FINANCE	19,741	26,076	26,382	24,647	21,499	21,799
GRAND TOTAL	422,469	1,058,328	1,105,478	1,083,640	1,016,886	1,001,823

[2] Furniture included in Timber.

TABLE VII

Number of Assessments in Trade Groups.   Corporate Enterprises

	1909 (1911–12)	1927 (1928–29)	1932 (1933–34)	1936 (1937–38)	1937 (1938–39)	1938 (1939–40)
Coal Mines	827	1,017	841	725	720	640
Iron Mines	48	40	29	31	46	36
Other Mines	133	102	90	103	78	57
Quarries	570	904	957	892	1,057	1,000
EXTRACTION	*1,578*	*2,063*	*1,917*	*1,751*	*1,901*	*1,733*
Cotton	1,124	1,481	843	1,047	1,004	842
Wool	508	940	826	1,076	925	835
Silk	62	211	234	263	318	268
Flax, Jute, Hemp	315	407	313	446	405	407
Lace	102	142	144	207	197	165
Hosiery	75	433	457	471	471	506
Misc. Textiles	95	167	186	261	266	206
Bleaching and Dyeing	218	432	385	362	388	331
TEXTILES	*2,499*	*4,213*	*3,388*	*4,133*	*3,974*	*3,560*
Iron and Steel	623	896	690	1,035	1,071	1,115
Machinery & Engineering	1,465	3,350	3,087	4,100	4,570	4,641
Shipbuilding	149	255	177	284	353	309
Combines of above	16	41	65	71	61	71
Rly. Carriage and Wagon	57	91	64	56	61	86
Motor and Cycle	351	829	807	842	992	1,047
Anchor, Chain, etc.	102	190	150	263	225	219
Small Arms, Tools, etc.	345	650	627	853	843	998
Wrought Iron & Steel Tube	412	744	679	925	1,080	899
Copper and Brass	218	474	364	516	558	531
Gold and Silver Plate	193	415	392	436	496	476
Lead, Tin, Zinc	76	127	137	167	172	161
Tinplate	48	87	83	104	114	104
Misc. Metals	112	205	194	385	322	281
METALS	*4,167*	*8,354*	*7,516*	*10,037*	*10,918*	*10,938*
Grain Milling	203	328	383	527	451	401
Biscuit & Bread (Wholesale)	69	163	235	299	254	330
Sugar and Glucose	15	85	72	102	67	82
Cocoa and Confectionery	164	366	388	401	341	401
Misc. Foods	392	666	761	871	871	823
Brewing	1,181 }	862	815	798	823	833
Distilling		92	60	68	98	78
Mineral Waters, etc.		301	246	257	267	272
Tobacco	60	100	142	128	138	113
FOOD, DRINK & TOBACCO	*2,084*	*2,963*	*3,102*	*3,451*	*3,310*	*3,333*
Fine Chemicals	377	818	854	1,021	981	1,082
Patent Medicines	58	105	106	123	122	110
Soap and Candles	89	142	153	105	130	181
Fertilizers, Explosives, etc.	680	1,078	1,093	1,153	1,169	1,169
CHEMICALS	*1,204*	*2,143*	*2,206*	*2,402*	*2,402*	*2,542*

	1909 (1911–12)	1927 (1928–29)	1932 (1933–34)	1936 (1937–38)	1937 (1938–39)	1938 (1939–40)
Leather and Rubber ..	451	918	813	1,033	1,000	988
Boots and Shoes ..	172	581	626	550	525	445
Misc. Clothing ..	465	1,616	1,830	2,218	2,453	2,418
Paper-making	178	343	374	438	488	398
Printing & Bookbinding	887	1,775	1,824	2,264	2,284	2,289
Publishing & Newspapers	818	1,119	1,047	1,361	1,326	1,297
Stationery	208	551	474	740	845	705
Furniture	2	445	422	565	610	600
Pottery, China, etc. ..	137	261	169	227	322	277
Glass	109	149	157	225	270	245
Instruments	340	928	999	1,083	1,028	1,198
Manufactures n.e.s. ..	242	600	519	675	675	624
OTHER MANUFACTURING	4,007[2]	9,286	9,254	11,379	11,826	11,484
Building & Contracting	531	2,149	2,644	3,734	3,750	3,789
Bricks, Cement, etc. ..	651	1,152	1,079	1,360	1,345	1,226
Timber	723[2]	1,072	1,016	1,417	1,413	1,447
BUILDING	1,905[2]	4,373	4,739	6,511	6,508	6,462
Gas	1,525	1,432	1,288	1,082	1,022	1,092
Water..	1,872	1,695	1,692	1,536	1,407	1,381
Electricity	473	850	833	715	700	650
PUBLIC UTILITIES ..	3,870	3,977	3,813	3,333	3,129	3,123
MANUFACTURING INDUSTRY	19,736	35,309	34,018	41,246	42,067	41,442
Wholesale Distribution ..	3,627	10,444	10,006	12,036	12,836	12,056
Hotels, Inns, etc. ..	1,171	1,442	1,448	1,716	1,796	1,746
Retail (purely distributive)	2,774	7,829	9,824	12,380	12,816	12,781
Retail (semi-industrial) ..	2,147	5,863	7,031	9,293	10,008	10,013
DISTRIBUTION	9,719	25,578	28,309	35,425	37,456	36,596
Docks, Canals ..	329	333	327	255	270	240
Shipping	1,558	954	658	918	984	950
Ships' Managers ..	39	150	117	140	140	155
Railways	168	112	104	37	33	35
Road Transport ..	763	2,587	2,912	3,627	4,212	4,077
Telephones	14	21	31	35	40	41
TRANSPORT	2,871	4,157	4,149	5,012	5,679	5,498
Law	5	18	22	50	25	30
Medicine and Dentistry	132	63	89	85	92	105
Literature and Art ..	10	62	76	155	120	125
Music and Drama ..	13	19	30	70	56	70
Accountancy ..	—	29	28	50	70	55
Engineering, Architecture	50	151	137	190	215	275
Other Professions ..	330	907	910	1,100	1,055	1,340
PROFESSIONS	540	1,249	1,292	1,700	1,633	2,000
Public Amusements ..	1,523	4,167	3,891	3,704	4,000	4,180
Fishing and Trawling ..	226	235	175	215	217	193
Markets, Tolls, etc. ..	2,154	1,777	1,667	1,135	1,155	1,055
Misc. profits n.e.s. ..	3,545	8,186	8,627	9,289	9,425	9,555
MISC. PROFITS	7,448	14,365	14,360	14,343	14,797	14,983
U.K. Total (excl. Finance)	41,892	82,721	84,045	99,477	103,533	102,252

	1909 (1911–12)	1927 (1928–29)	1932 (1933–34)	1936 (1937–38)	1937 (1938–39)	1938 (1939–40)
Rlys. and Transport O.U.K.	239	198	123	117	99	104
Cables, Telegraphs ..	43	39	19	27	27	12
Mineral Properties ..	597	297	245	263	294	231
Oil Concessions ..	63	77	60	57	46	31
Public Utilities ..	50	52	72	62	53	63
Land & Mortgage Concerns	183	163	139	156	169	120
Plantations	773	1,006	397	1,063	1,003	898
Banks..	58	23	28	42	20	39
Other Concerns ..	413	423	437	524	429	390
ADVENTURES O.U.K. ..	2,419	2,278	1,520	2,311	2,140	1,888
British Banks	134 ⎫	125	118	121	115	111
Foreign Banks in U.K. ..	⎬	31	32	31	24	24
Insurance	450 ⎭	764	854	901	867	1,052
Stockbrokers and Jobbers	25	106	112	211	203	209
Finance Companies and Bill-brokers	1,436	1,823	1,675	2,028	1,936	1,747
Other Brokers & Agents	655	1,345	1,357	1,759	1,684	1,753
FINANCE	2,700	4,194	4,148	5,051	4,829	4,896
GRAND TOTAL	47,011	89,193	89,713	106,839	110,502	109,036

[2] Furniture included in Timber.

TABLE VIII

Number of Assessments in Trade Groups.   Non-Corporate Enterprises

	1909 (1911–12)	1927 (1928–29)	1932 (1933–34)	1936 (1937–38)	1937 (1938–39)	1938 (1939–40)
Coal Mines	606	606	397	225	290	300
Iron Mines	30	30	21	25	27	20
Other Mines	140	59	51	53	53	55
Quarries	3,561	2,247	1,977	1,530	1,290	1,310
EXTRACTION	4,337	2,942	2,446	1,833	1,660	1,685
Cotton	712	450	311	265	251	275
Wool	1,144	970	779	635	618	495
Silk	112	260	238	205	187	133
Flax, Jute, Hemp ..	641	681	516	638	402	502
Lace	531	339	263	215	194	130
Hosiery	243	537	468	364	295	351
Misc. Textiles	311	305	250	225	180	190
Bleaching and Dyeing ..	461	362	250	222	177	197
TEXTILES	4,155	3,904	3,075	2,769	2,304	2,273

	1909 (1911–12)	1927 (1928–29)	1932 (1933–34)	1936 (1937–38)	1937 (1938–39)	1938 (1939–40)
Iron and Steel ..	670	741	630	680	570	560
Machinery & Engineering	1,860	4,738	4,370	3,935	3,635	3,115
Shipbuilding ..	146	539	527	480	430	420
Combines of above ..	4	—	—	11	10	—
Rly. Carriage and Wagon	25	49	48	50	15	30
Motor and Cycle ..	417	1,517	1,272	1,185	922	985
Anchor, Chain, etc. ..	210	311	225	240	210	190
Small Arms, Tools, etc. ..	845	2,010	1,534	1,260	1,045	1,275
Wrought Iron & Steel Tube	652	1,179	979	1,075	1,020	995
Copper and Brass ..	565	852	700	570	615	465
Gold and Silver Plate ..	1,049	1,516	1,324	1,177	977	905
Lead, Tin, Zinc ..	126	117	115	70	65	65
Tinplate	13	167	137	105	90	95
Misc. Metals	258	424	345	300	275	270
METALS	6,840	14,160	12,206	11,138	9,879	9,370
Grain Milling	1,300	1,716	1,541	1,446	1,132	1,010
Biscuit & Bread (Wholesale)	62	232	204	135	173	195
Sugar and Glucose ..	31	118	114	195	153	153
Cocoa and Confectionery	328	456	417	403	293	307
Misc. Foods	716	1,029	988	935	730	748
Brewing	⎫	746	587	440	457	438
Distilling	1,740 ⎬	25	13	30	20	15
Mineral Waters, etc. ..	⎭	749	558	276	260	219
Tobacco	168	140	128	110	101	105
FOOD, DRINK & TOBACCO	4,345	5,211	4,550	3,970	3,319	3,190
Fine Chemicals ..	413	478	487	443	430	426
Patent Medicines ..	104	76	79	90	70	55
Soap and Candles ..	114	129	143	80	95	50
Fertilizers, Explosives, etc.	820	888	788	705	704	540
CHEMICALS	1,451	1,571	1,497	1,318	1,299	1,071
Leather and Rubber ..	1,458	1,899	1,478	1,335	1,120	975
Boots and Shoes ..	805	1,784	1,302	1,060	620	695
Misc. Clothing ..	3,025	6,781	5,858	4,864	3,923	3,530
Paper-making ..	125	196	182	160	140	142
Printing & Bookbinding	3,079	5,981	5,761	5,420	4,665	4,760
Publishing & Newspapers	693	721	651	583	600	571
Stationery	510	949	867	830	765	740
Furniture	[2]	2,853	2,412	1,745	1,497	1,486
Pottery, China, etc. ..	254	302	186	205	180	168
Glass	255	266	227	185	160	200
Instruments	1,117	2,282	2,105	1,930	1,460	2,435
Manufactures n.e.s. ..	697	964	888	710	654	635
OTHER MANUFACTURING	12,000[2]	24,978	21,917	19,027	15,784	16,337
Building & Contracting	8,753	14,837	14,783	14,745	13,777	12,497
Bricks, Cement, etc. ..	1,298	1,105	1,040	920	815	720
Timber ·.. ..	3,981[2]	4,355	4,040	3,795	2,940	2,750
BUILDING	14,032[2]	20,297	19,863	19,460	17,532	15,967
Gas	101	66	45	43	37	31
Water..	793	371	368	247	275	205
Electricity	18	190	220	230	235	160
PUBLIC UTILITIES ..	912	627	633	520	547	396

	1909 (1911–12)	1927 (1928–29)	1932 (1933–34)	1936 (1937–38)	1937 (1938–39)	1938 (1939–40)
MANUFACTURING INDUSTRY	43,735	70,748	63,741	58,202	50,664	48,604
Wholesale Distribution ..	27,533	47,902	44,085	40,535	36,150	35,435
Hotels, Inns, etc. ..	45,082	77,873	75,119	72,470	59,230	58,200
Retail (purely distributive)	79,451	289,127	312,274	302,960	294,870	289,055
Retail (semi-industrial) ..	45,410	238,582	259,095	255,020	239,130	233,185
DISTRIBUTION	197,476	653,484	690,573	670,985	629,380	615,875
Docks, Canals ..	198	151	144	155	90	125
Shipping	1,717	959	735	730	640	625
Ships' managers ..	615	374	245	191	166	161
Railways	4	—	—	—	—	—
Road Transport ..	3,387	27,577	31,792	31,860	25,795	30,035
Telephones	—	—	—	—	—	—
TRANSPORT	5,921	29,061	32,916	32,936	26,691	30,946
Law	13,309	12,688	12,473	12,575	12,360	12,390
Medicine and Dentistry ..	22,146	30,867	32,130	31,710	31,025	30,665
Literature and Art ..	5,246	7,664	8,659	8,535	8,105	7,915
Music and Drama ..	4,477	7,770	9,178	9,040	8,725	7,785
Accountancy	3,448	7,804	8,492	9,584	9,119	9,619
Engineering, Architecture	6,635	8,330	8,036	8,205	7,905	7,595
Other Professions ..	19,651	30,472	34,532	33,515	31,075	30,560
PROFESSIONS	74,912	105,595	113,500	113,164	108,314	106,529
Public Amusements ..	1,288	4,453	4,664	4,155	3,945	3,690
Fishing and Trawling ..	1,557	2,997	2,428	2,370	1,705	1,705
Markets, Tolls, etc. ..	2,348	3,000	1,948	1,620	1,140	950
Misc. profits, n.e.s. ..	26,059	73,749	80,282	71,445	65,595	65,245
MISC. PROFITS	31,252	84,199	89,322	79,590	72,385	71,590
U.K. Total (excl. Finance)	357,633	946,029	992,498	956,710	889,094	875,229
Rlys. & Transport O.U.K.	171	4	2	—	—	—
Cables, Telegraphs ..	3	41	14	—	—	—
Mineral Properties ..	17	33	19	—	—	—
Oil Concessions ..	6	1	—	—	—	—
Public Utilities ..	17	30	27	—	—	—
Land & Mortgage Concerns	11	110	116	—	—	—
Plantations	157	188	89	65	125	120
Banks..	2	12	11	—	—	—
Other Concerns ..	400	805	755	430	495	535
ADVENTURES O.U.K. ..	784	1,224	1,033	495	620	655
British Banks	47 ⎫	40	37	39	47	31
Foreign Banks in U.K. ..	⎬	—	—	—	—	—
Insurance	724 ⎭	5,105	5,890	5,050	4,765	4,840
Stockbrokers and Jobbers	3,385	2,721	2,462	2,347	1,738	1,742
Finance Companies, Bill-						
Brokers	2,349	2,489	2,044	1,885	1,530	1,490
Other Brokers and Agents	10,536	11,527	11,801	10,275	8,590	8,800
FINANCE	17,041	21,882	22,234	19,596	16,670	16,903
GRAND TOTAL	375,458	969,135	1,015,765	976,801	906,384	892,787

[2] Furniture included in Timber.

TABLE IX

Average Gross True Income per Assessment. All Enterprises £ (to nearest £50)

	1909 (1911–12)	1927 (1928–29)	1932 (1933–34)	1936 (1937–38)	1937 (1938–39)	1938 (1939–40)
Coal Mines	11,850	7,500	10,250	22,350	22,300	25,100
Iron Mines	3,400 }	6,050	3,150	4,000	7,900	11,300
Other Mines		4,650	2,100	5,450	6,550	4,250
Quarries	300	1,100	800	1,750	2,100	1,800
EXTRACTION	3,300	3,350	3,550	7,400	8,100	8,450
Cotton	4,700	6,150	2,800	5,050	7,680	6,100
Wool	3,350	4,650	3,050	6,500	5,000	3,800
Silk		12,050	4,400	9,550	7,750	4,700
Flax, Jute, Hemp		2,100	1,050	2,000	2,750	1,150
Lace	2,400 }	1,200	750	1,150	1,150	1,150
Hosiery		3,200	2,150	3,950	4,300	3,300
Misc. Textiles		2,200	1,600	2,350	2,300	2,600
Bleaching and Dyeing	3,600	5,000	3,500	3,400	4,250	2,650
TEXTILES	3,400	4,600	2,500	4,550	4,900	3,500
Iron and Steel		3,150	2,450	7,050	11,600	9,600
Machinery & Engineering		3,350	2,050	5,350	7,000	7,900
Shipbuilding	4,250 }	1,700	550	3,350	3,700	8,750
Combines of above		43,700	21,250	67,050	113,350	131,600
Rly. Carriage and Wagon		7,800	5,800	11,800	21,900	15,500
Motor and Cycle		4,050	2,650	8,250	9,650	8,600
Anchor, Chain, etc.		1,400	1,600	4,500	5,900	5,650
Small Arms, Tools, etc.		1,200	1,100	3,350	3,900	3,650
Wrought Iron & Steel Tube	1,650 }	2,950	2,050	4,700	6,500	6,400
Copper and Brass		1,700	1,250	4,600	4,400	4,250
Gold and Silver Plate		900	650	1,350	1,350	1,350
Lead, Tin, Zinc		5,400	6,650	16,050	22,050	20,100
Tinplate		2,350	3,050	11,350	11,400	5,950
Misc. Metals		1,000	1,200	3,600	5,550	3,950
METALS	2,850	2,750	1,950	5,450	7,150	7,350
Grain Milling		1,300	2,200	2,650	3,000	3,000
Biscuit & Bread (Wholesale)		8,700	5,350	4,600	5,600	4,250
Sugar and Glucose	2,350[1] }	18,100	10,300	12,800	16,000	13,050
Cocoa and Confectionery		4,550	4,300	5,050	5,400	5,700
Misc. Foods		4,400	4,250	9,350	9,050	7,900
Brewing		15,400	13,450	20,300	19,600	20,500
Distilling	5,700[1] }	43,550	46,200	55,900	48,350	62,450
Mineral Waters		1,850	1,450	3,050	2,100	2,500
Tobacco	12,300	51,000	37,750	59,600	64,250	70,350
FOOD, DRINK & TOBACCO	4,250	7,950	6,950	10,550	11,450	11,400
Fine Chemicals		6,400	6,800	9,850	11,800	9,000
Patent Medicines		5,600	4,250	6,650	7,600	5,900
Soap and Candles	3,400 }	20,550	13,550	23,950	19,400	22,750
Fertilizers, Explosives		4,850	5,250	7,450	8,000	7,950
CHEMICALS	3,400	6,600	6,400	9,150	10,150	9,250

	1909 (1911–12)	1927 (1928–29)	1932 (1933–34)	1936 (1937–38)	1937 (1938–39)	1938 (1939–40)
Leather and Rubber	⎫	3,000	1,950	3,850	3,550	3,500
Boots and Shoes	1,200 ⎬	1,650	1,150	2,000	2,250	1,950
Misc. Clothing	⎭	1,250	750	950	1,350	1,100
Paper-making	⎫	7,350	9,900	14,350	14,450	16,250
Printing, Bookbinding	1,500 ⎬	950	700	1,050	1,150	1,150
Publishing, Newspapers		7,550	4,950	7,250	6,750	5,550
Stationery	⎭	1,900	1,650	2,400	3,350	3,400
Furniture	²	950	500	1,100	1,100	900
Pottery, China, etc.	⎫	2,500	2,450	4,300	2,800	3,500
Glass	1,200 ⎬	3,800	2,950	9,250	7,400	8,050
Instruments		1,700	850	1,650	1,900	1,350
Manufactures n.e.s.	⎭	2,800	3,300	3,950	5,000	3,800
OTHER MANUFACTURING	$1,350^2$	1,950	1,450	2,400	2,600	2,300
Building and Contracting	⎫	1,000	750	1,050	1,100	1,150
Bricks, Cement, etc.	600^2 ⎬	3,150	2,700	5,300	4,950	5,950
Timber	⎭	750	600	1,300	1,500	1,050
BUILDING	600^2	1,150	900	1,450	1,500	1,550
Gas	5,150	10,250	10,950	11,900	12,700	11,900
Water	2,300	4,200	5,050	6,650	7,200	6,500
Electricity	$8,350^5$	15,850	24,250	31,000	34,200	39,900
PUBLIC UTILITIES	3,900	8,800	11,350	14,150	15,650	15,900
MANUFACTURING INDUSTRY	2,200	3,050	2,550	4,250	4,950	4,800
Wholesale Distribution	1,450	1,450	950	1,550	1,800	1,550
Hotels, Inns, etc.	⎫	350	250	350	400	350
Retail (purely distributive)	300 ⎬	350	300	400	400	350
Retail (semi-industrial)	⎭	350	250	300	300	300
DISTRIBUTION	500	450	350	450	450	450
Docks, Canals	7,700 ⎫	11,350	12,650	14,550	18,150	17,100
Shipping	$4,150^5$ ⎬	12,100	6,700	14,450	23,400	19,700
Ships' managers	⎭	1,800	1,700	2,450	2,700	3,600
Railways	260,450	331,400	228,700	739,950	904,200	786,650
Road Transport	$1,700^5$	750	700	1,000	1,350	1,150
Telephones	$82,150^5$	4,700	8,650	5,150	6,300	4,300
TRANSPORT	8,350	2,700	1,750	2,450	3,600	2,850
Law	⎫	1,350	1,250	1,500	1,550	1,400
Medicine and Dentistry		750	750	900	950	950
Literature and Art		350	300	400	350	350
Music and Drama	400 ⎬	300	250	350	400	400
Accountancy		1,050	1,000	1,150	1,050	950
Engineering, Architecture		800	650	950	**1,100**	1,100
Other Professions	⎭	450	350	450	500	450
PROFESSIONS	400	700	600	750	800	800
Public Amusements	³	800	1,000	1,250	1,550	1,400
Fishing and Trawling	500^5	450	350	800	950	750
Markets, Tolls, etc.	250	350	450	600	700	550
Misc. profits n.e.s.	$150^{3,5}$	200	200	200	200	250
MISC. PROFITS	200	250	250	300	350	400

	1909 (1911–12)	1927 (1928–29)	1932 (1933–34)	1936 (1937–38)	1937 (1938–39)	1938 (1939–40)
All U.K. Industries (excl. Finance)	900	800	600	900	1,050	1,000
Rlys. & Transport O.U.K.	48,700	151,650	78,200	83,150	117,900	91,650
Cables, Telegraphs		58,850	35,500	67,850	65,500	122,650
Mineral Properties	28,250	33,000	23,650	68,950	79,900	88,750
Oil Concessions		162,400	183,350	271,500	487,950	559,600
Public Utilities	[4]	18,800	14,200	14,100	19,900	12,100
Land & Mortgage Concerns	[4]	7,000	4,050	8,250	7,400	9,000
Plantations	7,350	17,900	4,400	10,950	15,550	11,450
Banks..	68,350	127,950	40,800	101,600	184,650	75,550
Other Concerns	9,800[4,5]	15,550	11,900	25,400	29,350	29,900
ADVENTURES O.U.K.	19,650	30,650	19,000	31,400	39,850	36,550
British Banks		121,350	29,250	−78,450	−90,600	−90,700
Foreign Banks in U.K.	9,450	13,000	14,150	17,150	16,650	10,500
Insurance		1,900	1,900	2,500	2,400	2,250
Stockbrokers and Jobbers	2,750	5,500	4,800	6,200	1,850	100
Finance Companies, Bill-brokers	1,150	2,750	2,750	3,100	1,600	900
Other Brokers and Agents		650	650	300	850	300
FINANCE	2,000	2,550	1,850	1,400	800	300
ALL INDUSTRIES	1,100	950	700	1,000	1,150	1,050

For 1909:
[1] Sugar and Gluclose included in Brewing, etc.
[2] Furniture included in Building.
[3] Public Amusements included in Misc. profits n.e.s.
[4] Public Utilities and Land, etc., included in Other Concerns O.U.K.
[5] Estimated on the basis of the gross *assessment* in 1911–12.

TABLE X

Average Gross True Income per Assessment. Corporate Enterprises £

	1927 (1928–29)	1932 (1933–34)	1936 (1937–38)	1937 (1938–40)	1938 (1939–40)
Coal Mines	11,290	14,580	29,120	31,080	36,390
Iron Mines ..	9,990	5,150	5,870	10,350	17,110
Other Mines	7,250	3,030	7,820	10,740	8,000
Quarries	2,440	1,600	3,050	3,780	3,310
EXTRACTION	7,190	7,420	14,180	14,570	15,970
Cotton	7,610	3,620	6,080	9,200	7,790
Wool	7,250	4,820	9,190	7,700	5,520
Silk	25,520	8,390	16,590	11,980	6,690
Flax, Jute, Hemp	4,510	2,240	4,000	4,710	1,950
Lace	2,370	1,040	1,630	1,670	1,590
Hosiery	4,810	3,410	5,670	6,220	4,110
Misc. Textiles	4,850	2,870	3,580	3,310	4,410
Bleaching and Dyeing	7,890	5,140	4,370	5,430	3,630
TEXTILES	7,580	4,110	6 760	7,130	5,110

I

	1927 (1928–29)	1932 (1933–34)	1936 (1937–38)	1937 (1938–39)	1938 (1939–40)
Iron and Steel	4,800	4,050	10,870	16,480	13,900
Machinery and Engineering	7,250	4,280	9,930	11,900	12,820
Shipbuilding	4,310	1,260	7,670	7,320	20,180
Combines of above	43,720	21,280	79,560	131,890	133,030
Rly. Carriage and Wagon	11,720	9,800	22,020	26,660	20,420
Motor and Cycle	10,580	6,230	19,250	18,100	16,240
Anchor, Chain, etc. ..	2,470	3,260	7,470	10,350	9,370
Small Arms, Tools, etc.	3,580	3,040	7,420	7,840	7,600
Wrought Iron and Steel Tube	6,670	4,360	9,410	11,930	12,600
Copper and Brass	3,400	2,870	8,970	8,520	7,310
Gold and Silver Plate	2,050	1,360	3,200	2,710	2,490
Lead, Tin, Zinc	9,790	11,860	22,480	30,060	28,050
Tinplate	5,430	7,220	21,830	20,080	10,890
Misc. Metals	1,800	2,630	5,830	9,440	7,070
METALS	*6,420*	*4,380*	*10,810*	*12,880*	*13,080*
Grain Milling	5,820	9,230	7,890	8,770	8,940
Biscuit & Bread (Wholesale) ..	18,450	9,090	6,400	9,040	6,500
Sugar and Glucose ..	42,180	25,650	36,180	50,910	36,160
Cocoa and Confectionery	9,360	8,380	9,750	9,640	9,550
Misc. Foods	9,800	9,160	18,680	15,950	14,610
Brewing	27,400	22,580	30,400	29,830	30,760
Distilling ..	54,180	55,940	80,000	57,750	71,780
Mineral Waters, etc. ..	5,070	3,620	5,650	3,330	3,950
Tobacco	120,170	70,710	110,280	110,340	135,160
FOOD, DRINK AND TOBACCO ..	*20,450*	*16,260*	*21,790*	*22,100*	*21,640*
Fine Chemicals	9,480	10,220	13,730	16,690	12,330
Patent Medicines	7,520	6,240	8,820	10,890	7,750
Soap and Candles	38,390	25,800	41,800	33,160	28,870
Fertilizers, Explosives, etc.	8,030	8,510	11,200	12,220	11,180
CHEMICALS ..	*10,570*	*10,260*	*13,490*	*15,110*	*12,780*
Leather and Rubber	7,540	4,490	7,820	6,690	6,230
Boots and Shoes	4,490	2,560	4,750	4,200	3,860
Misc. Clothing	3,460	1,690	1,780	2,430	1,780
Paper-making	10,920	14,290	19,030	17,910	21,010
Printing and Bookbinding	2,400	1,690	2,580	2,340	2,430
Publishing and Newspapers	11,220	7,370	9,450	9,040	7,500
Stationery	3,910	3,500	3,970	5,760	6,180
Furniture	3,040	1,160	2,820	2,280	1,970
Pottery, China, etc.	4,340	4,350	7,010	3,860	5,420
Glass	8,970	6,300	16,200	10,960	13,760
Instruments	4,500	1,860	3,600	3,830	3,400
Manufactures n.e.s.	5,470	8,260	7,460	9,270	7,140
OTHER MANUFACTURING	*5,290*	*3,730*	*5,310*	*5,210*	*4,770*
Building and Contracting	2,710	1,830	2,420	2,500	2,660
Bricks, Cement, etc.	5,230	4,790	8,390	7,480	9,130
Timber	1,770	1,490	3,160	3,040	2,080
BUILDING ..	*3,140*	*2,430*	*3,830*	*3,650*	*3,760*
Gas	10,700	11,320	12,360	13,160	12,250
Water	5,110	6,140	7,720	8,610	7,420
Electricity ..	19,310	30,560	40,920	45,600	49,640
PUBLIC UTILITIES	*10,160*	*13,230*	*16,350*	*18,370*	*17,890*

		1927 (1928–29)	1932 (1933–34)	1936 (1937–38)	1937 (1938–39)	1938 (1939–40)
MANUFACTURING INDUSTRY	..	*7,710*	*6,360*	*9,310*	*10,010*	*9,670*
Wholesale Distribution	..	4,470	2,910	4,510	4,570	3,940
Hotels, Inns, etc. ..	..	3,380	1,570	2,680	2,870	2,370
Retail (purely distributive)	..	2,750	2,480	3,360	3,490	3,070
Retail (semi-industrial)	..	1,490	1,050	1,530	1,320	1,310
DISTRIBUTION	..	*3,200*	*2,230*	*3,240*	*3,250*	*2,840*
Docks, Canals ..	..	16,280	18,110	22,660	23,990	25,750
Shipping ..	..	23,290	13,510	25,200	37,640	31,850
Ships' managers	..	3,190	2,140	3,080	2,630	3,760
Railways ..	..	331,480	228,830	739,950	904,180	786,630
Road Transport	..	4,930	5,170	6,110	6,510	6,500
Telephones	..	4,710	8,680	5,140	6,280	4,320
TRANSPORT	..	*18,790*	*13,060*	*15,770*	*17,860*	*16,600*
Law ..	..	390	310	520	80	1,170
Medicine and Dentistry	..	240	840	530	470	260
Literature and Art ..	..	750	450	1,510	520	310
Music and Drama ..	..	640	460	370	520	460
Accountancy ..	..	410	590	4,380	1,370	310
Engineering, Architecture	..	1,380	650	800	1,530	1,450
Other Professions ..	..	1,120	800	1,170	1,470	780
PROFESSIONS	..	*1,060*	*750*	*1,170*	*1,290*	*800*
Public Amusements ..	..	1,210	1,830	2,210	2,620	2,210
Fishing and Trawling	..	3,280	3,280	7,060	6,400	5,060
Markets, Tolls, etc. ..	..	790	880	1,340	1,200	890
Misc. profits n.e.s.	..	620	840	630	710	1,240
MISC. PROFITS	..	*860*	*1,140*	*1,190*	*1,350*	*1,530*
All U.K. Industries (excl. Finance)		*5,570*	*4,350*	*6,250*	*6,700*	*6,340*
Rlys. and Transport O.U.K.	..	154,690	79,550	83,140	117,880	91,670
Cables, Telegraphs	..	120,580	61,470	67,850	65,480	122,670
Mineral Properties	..	36,660	25,500	68,940	79,880	88,750
Oil Concessions	..	164,530	183,350	271,510	487,930	559,580
Public Utilities	..	29,230	19,550	14,110	19,920	12,100
Land and Mortgage Concerns		11,290	7,060	8,230	7,400	8,980
Plantations ..	..	20,790	5,110	11,580	17,150	12,840
Banks ..	..	194,560	56,730	101,600	184,650	75,540
Other Concerns	..	44,870	31,890	45,960	62,590	69,870
ADVENTURES O.U.K.	..	*46,800*	*31,680*	*38,070*	*51,130*	*48,950*
British Banks	..	147,660	30,730	−110,610	−131,390	−117,300
Foreign Banks in U.K.	..	13,000	14,150	17,160	16,630	10,500
Insurance ..	..	12,260	11,110	11,910	11,770	8,850
Stockbrokers and Jobbers		460	590	5,100	−11,340	1,610
Finance Companies, Bill-brokers		5,170	4,160	5,760	2,440	1,380
Other Brokers and Agents	..	1,970	2,730	−1,020	2,290	−1,180
FINANCE ..	..	*9,620*	*5,860*	*1,750*	*370*	*−570*
ALL INDUSTRIES	..	*6,810*	*4,880*	*6,720*	*7,290*	*6,770*

TABLE XI

Average Gross True Income per Assessment.   Non-corporate Enterprises £

	1927 (1928–29)	1932 (1933–34)	1936 (1937–38)	1937 (1938–39)	1938 (1939–40)
Coal Mines	1,150	1,140	560	540	1,080
Iron Mines ..	790	350	1,680	3,780	800
Other Mines	200	420	890	320	360
Quarries	530	380	1,000	730	680
EXTRACTION	*660*	*500*	*950*	*730*	*740*
Cotton	1,400	670	930	1,610	910
Wool	2,080	1,210	1,990	1,010	900
Silk	1,140	430	520	620	630
Flax, Jute, Hemp	670	340	570	730	540
Lace	700	580	710	550	640
Hosiery	1,840	870	1,780	1,230	2,170
Misc. Textiles	760	630	870	840	620
Bleaching and Dyeing	1,600	950	1,830	1,730	1,010
TEXTILES	*1,400*	*780*	*1,220*	*1,030*	*970*
Iron and Steel	1,160	720	1,200	2,440	970
Machinery and Engineering	600	440	610	790	620
Shipbuilding	480	310	780	720	310
Combines of above	—	—	−13,640	200	—
Rly. Carriage and Wagon	400	410	380	2,530	1,330
Motor and Cycle	520	370	450	540	500
Anchor, Chain, etc. ..	720	520	1,240	1,100	1,360
Small Arms, Tools, etc.	420	340	580	750	580
Wrought Iron and Steel Tube	610	430	680	740	810
Copper and Brass	750	410	670	700	790
Gold and Silver Plate	570	450	660	650	720
Lead, Tin, Zinc	680	460	760	830	460
Tinplate	750	500	930	430	510
Misc. Metals	630	370	730	1,030	690
METALS	*600*	*430*	*650*	*840*	*650*
Grain Milling	440	480	730	730	660
Biscuit and Bread (Wholesale)	1,850	1,050	620	560	470
Sugar and Glucose	740	620	570	730	670
Cocoa and Confectionery	700	520	410	470	660
Misc. Foods	930	500	660	800	570
Brewing	1,550	770	2,040	1,180	980
Distilling	4,450	1,230	1,270	2,350	14,000
Mineral Waters, etc. ..	520	480	590	830	740
Tobacco	1,560	1,160	620	1,330	630
FOOD, DRINK AND TOBACCO	*850*	*570*	*810*	*810*	*740*
Fine Chemicals	1,160	770	840	660	540
Patent Medicines	2,920	1,610	3,690	1,830	2,200
Soap and Candles	870	460	500	610	540
Fertilizers, Explosives, etc.	1,040	710	1,380	1,010	920
CHEMICALS ..	*1,150*	*750*	*1,300*	*910*	*820*

	1927 (1928–29)	1932 (1933–34)	1936 (1937–38)	1937 (1938–39)	1938 (1939–40)
Leather and Rubber ..	830	550	770	740	700
Boots and Shoes	720	510	570	610	700
Misc. Clothing	710	460	570	640	640
Paper-making	1,080	850	1,540	2,300	2,940
Printing and Bookbinding ..	550	420	430	560	530
Publishing and Newspapers ..	1,870	1,100	2,100	1,730	1,060
Stationery	720	680	1,000	730	720
Furniture	640	380	560	630	480
Pottery, China, etc. ..	900	690	1,270	870	290
Glass	910	660	790	1,400	1,050
Instruments	570	390	580	570	350
Manufactures n.e.s. ..	1,110	420	590	550	550
OTHER MANUFACTURING ..	*720*	*470*	*630*	*680*	*590*
Building and Contracting ..	740	570	680	720	700
Bricks, Cement, etc. ..	980	590	760	790	580
Timber	500	370	640	740	540
BUILDING	*700*	*530*	*680*	*730*	*670*
Gas	300	−160	300	510	230
Water	80	80	130	110	150
Electricity	360	300	130	260	330
PUBLIC UTILITIES	*190*	*140*	*150*	*200*	*230*
MANUFACTURING INDUSTRY ..	*740*	*510*	*700*	*750*	*660*
Wholesale Distribution ..	780	490	700	800	740
Hotels, Inns, etc.	320	210	270	300	300
Retail (purely distributive) ..	300	230	250	250	250
Retail (semi-industrial) ..	330	250	280	270	270
DISTRIBUTION	*350*	*250*	*290*	*300*	*290*
Docks, Canals	430	290	1,180	600	500
Shipping	930	560	880	1,510	1,220
Ships' managers	1,270	1,530	2,010	2,740	3,460
Railways	—	—	—	—	—
Road Transport	370	310	430	500	410
Telephones	—	—	—	—	—
TRANSPORT	*400*	*330*	*450*	*540*	*440*
Law	1,350	1,250	1,490	1,540	1,390
Medicine and Dentistry ..	780	750	920	970	960
Literature and Art	340	280	370	360	340
Music and Drama	290	250	340	390	380
Accountancy	1,030	990	1,120	1,040	960
Engineering, Architecture ..	800	630	950	1,070	1,070
Other Professions	420	320	430	440	440
PROFESSIONS	*690*	*610*	*770*	*810*	*780*
Public Amusements	440	330	410	470	480
Fishing and Trawling ..	230	160	210	230	260
Markets, Tolls, etc.	80	80	120	220	150
Misc. profits n.e.s.	130	120	140	140	130
MISC. PROFITS	*150*	*130*	*150*	*160*	*150*
All U.K. Industries (excl. Finance)	*400*	*300*	*370*	*380*	*360*

	1927 (1928–29)	1932 (1933–34)	1936 (1937–38)	1937 (1938–39)	1938 (1939–40)
Railways & Transport O.U.K.	1,080	−4,080	—	—	—
Cables, Telegraphs	110	190	—	—	—
Mineral Properties ..	70	120	—	—	—
Oil Concessions ..	−230	—	—	—	—
Public Utilities ..	710	20	—	—	—
Land and Mortgage Concerns	710	410	—	—	—
Plantations ..	2,400	1,090	850	2,890	900
Banks ..	330	280	—	—	—
Other Concerns ..	150	360	300	530	750
ADVENTURES O.U.K. ..	*560*	*400*	*370*	*1,000*	*770*
British Banks ..	39,100	24,630	21,310	9,130	4,520
Foreign Banks in U.K. ..	—	—	—	—	—
Insurance ..	370	580	800	720	810
Stockbrokers and Jobbers	5,690	5,000	6,300	3,370	−90
Finance Companies and Bill-brokers ..	960	1,600	280	490	330
Other Brokers and Agents	470	380	510	540	610
FINANCE ..	*1,220*	*1,100*	*1,300*	*910*	*580*
ALL INDUSTRIES ..	*420*	*320*	*390*	*390*	*370*

TABLE XII
Index Numbers of Gross True Income.   All Enterprises

	1909 (1911–12)	1927 (1928–29)	1932 (1933–34)	1936 (1937–38)	1937 (1938–39)	1938 (1939–40)
Coal Mines ..	139	100.0	104.4	174.4	185.0	193.9
Iron Mines ..	102 ⎱	100.0	37.1	53.0	136.6	149.4
Other Mines ..	⎰	100.0	39.1	113.4	113.8	63.4
Quarries ..	35	100.0	67.1	124.7	144.8	123.1
EXTRACTION ..	*116*	*100.0*	*92.2*	*158.5*	*172.5*	*172.5*
Cotton ..	72	100.0	27.4	55.5	81.0	57.2
Wool ..	63	100.0	55.7	126.2	87.7	57.2
Silk ..	⎫	100.0	36.4	78.7	69.1	33.0
Flax, Jute, Hemp ..	⎪	100.0	38.4	93.8	96.2	46.5
Lace ..	47 ⎬	100.0	52.6	85.5	76.2	60.3
Hosiery ..	⎪	100.0	63.7	107.3	106.5	91.9
Misc. Textiles ..	⎭	100.0	66.3	108.7	99.2	98.7
Bleaching and Dyeing ..	61	100.0	55.6	49.8	60.5	35.0
TEXTILES ..	*60*	*100.0*	*43.6*	*83.7*	*82.1*	*54.6*
Iron and Steel ..	⎫	100.0	63.0	233.8	368.8	310.7
Machinery and Engineering	59 ⎬	100.0	55.8	158.9	211.0	226.4
Ship-building ..	⎪	100.0	28.3	188.5	213.5	470.0
Combines of above ..	⎭	100.0	77.1	307.0	449.3	521.8
Rly. Carriage and Wagon ..	⎫	100.0	59.6	115.3	153.2	165.4
Motor and Cycle ..	⎪	100.0	57.5	175.2	193.1	183.0
Anchor, Chain, etc. ..	⎪	100.0	87.2	325.9	368.9	333.0
Small Arms, Tools, etc. ..	⎪	100.0	76.6	222.6	233.2	262.5
Wrought Iron and Steel Tube	38 ⎬	100.0	59.6	166.0	240.1	213.5
Copper and Brass ..	⎪	100.0	59.1	222.8	230.7	189.0
Gold and Silver Plate ..	⎪	100.0	65.6	126.3	115.4	106.8
Lead, Tin, Zinc ..	⎪	100.0	126.8	287.8	394.9	343.6
Tinplate.. ..	⎪	100.0	111.7	396.0	389.3	197.3
Misc. Metals ..	⎭	100.0	100.2	387.3	522.6	341.8
METALS ..	*50*	*100.0*	*61.4*	*186.3*	*239.7*	*240.1*

	1909 (1911–12)	1927 (1928–29)	1932 (1933–34)	1936 (1937–38)	1937 (1938–39)	1938 (1939–40)
Grain Milling .. .. ⎫		100.0	160.4	195.8	179.9	160.0
Biscuit & Bread (Wholesale)		100.0	68.4	58.1	69.6	65.1
Sugar and Glucose .. 44[1] ⎬		100.0	52.2	103.5	95.9	83.5
Cocoa and Confectionery ..		100.0	92.6	108.9	91.5	107.7
Misc. Foods .. .. ⎭		100.0	99.7	225.6	193.4	166.3
Brewing .. .. ⎫		100.0	76.1	101.5	101.3	105.1
Distilling .. .. 48[1] ⎬		100.0	66.2	107.5	112.0	114.0
Mineral Waters, etc. .. ⎭		100.0	60.4	84.2	57.7	64.5
Tobacco 23		100.0	83.3	115.9	125.5	125.4
FOOD, DRINK AND TOBACCO 42		*100.0*	*81.6*	*120.6*	*116.7*	*114.5*
Fine Chemicals .. .. ⎫		100.0	109.5	173.2	200.5	163.3
Patent Medicines .. ⎪		100.0	78.0	140.0	144.0	96.2
Soap and Candles .. 37 ⎨		100.0	72.2	79.6	78.5	94.4
Fertilizers, Explosives, etc. ⎭		100.0	102.9	144.9	156.6	141.7
CHEMICALS 37		*100.0*	*97.1*	*139.5*	*153.2*	*136.4*
Leather and Rubber .. ⎫		100.0	52.5	107.2	88.4	80.5
Boots and Shoes .. 34 ⎬		100.0	58.0	82.5	66.2	56.5
Misc. Clothing .. .. ⎭		100.0	55.8	64.6	81.6	63.1
Paper-making .. ⎫		100.0	139.0	217.0	229.1	222.0
Printing and Bookbinding ⎪		100.0	72.7	108.4	105.9	107.3
Publishing and Newspapers 35 ⎨		100.0	60.7	101.3	93.7	74.3
Stationery .. .. ⎪		100.0	79.3	132.9	191.5	172.6
Furniture .. .. [2] ⎭		100.0	44.0	80.4	72.9	59.6
Pottery, China, etc. .. ⎫		100.0	61.4	131.7	99.6	110.4
Glass .. .. .. 30 ⎬		100.0	72.1	240.1	201.6	226.9
Instruments .. .. ⎪		100.0	49.0	91.7	87.1	89.8
Manufactures n.e.s. .. ⎭		100.0	107.0	125.2	152.1	110.5
OTHER MANUFACTURING .. 33[2]		*100.0*	*67.0*	*107.9*	*108.0*	*96.2*
Building and Contracting .. ⎫		100.0	78.6	113.0	114.4	111.5
Bricks, Cement, etc. .. 30[2] ⎬		100.0	81.2	170.4	150.8	163.4
Timber .. .. ⎭		100.0	74.4	169.9	159.4	110.9
BUILDING .. .. 30[2]		*100.0*	*78.6*	*135.8*	*130.2*	*124.5*
Gas 55		100.0	95.0	87.2	87.8	87.2
Water 70		100.0	119.9	136.8	139.7	118.2
Electricity .. .. 25[5]		100.0	154.8	177.7	194.0	196.1
PUBLIC UTILITIES .. 46		*100.0*	*124.7*	*134.7*	*142.1*	*138.1*
MANUFACTURING INDUSTRY 43		*100.0*	*76.6*	*130.8*	*141.6*	*133.3*
Wholesale Distribution .. 54		100.0	60.1	98.2	104.2	87.6
Hotels, Inns, etc... .. ⎫		100.0	60.9	81.6	77.8	72.0
Retail (purely distributive) 24 ⎬		100.0	88.1	108.8	109.2	101.0
Retail (semi-industrial) .. ⎭		100.0	83.4	97.6	90.9	86.7
DISTRIBUTION 32		*100.0*	*76.6*	*100.2*	*99.7*	*90.6*

	1909 (1911–12)	1927 (1928–29)	1932 (1933–34)	1936 (1937–38)	1937 (1938–39)	1938 (1939–40)
Docks, Canals	74	100.0	108.7	108.6	119.0	113.8
Shipping	68⁵ ⎫	100.0	40.2	102.9	164.5	134.2
Ships' managers	⎭	100.0	65.5	85.5	86.4	119.5
Railways	121	100.0	64.1	73.8	80.4	74.2
Road Transport	30⁵	100.0	108.3	155.5	175.4	167.9
Telephones	1,162⁵	100.0	270.7	181.8	253.5	178.8
TRANSPORT	*82*	*100.0*	*72.3*	*104.6*	*129.0*	*116.7*
Law	⎫	100.0	91.3	109.2	110.8	100.8
Medicine and Dentistry	⎪	100.0	100.8	122.2	126.1	123.4
Literature and Art	⎪	100.0	90.5	127.9	111.5	100.8
Music and Drama	41 ⎬	100.0	101.5	138.6	152.2	133.4
Accountancy	⎪	100.0	104.9	136.1	119.6	115.5
Engineering & Architecture	⎪	100.0	74.3	115.9	128.2	124.2
Other Professions	⎭	100.0	86.3	113.1	111.4	104.9
PROFESSIONS	*41*	*100.0*	*93.6*	*119.1*	*119.6*	*113.5*
Public Amusements	³	100.0	123.7	141.1	176.3	157.3
Fishing and Trawling	58⁵	100.0	65.2	138.6	122.0	96.9
Markets, Tolls, etc.	71	100.0	99.9	104.7	100.6	66.2
Misc. profits, n.e.s.	25³,⁵	100.0	113.9	107.6	110.6	140.3
MISC. PROFITS	*30*	*100.0*	*112.9*	*118.8*	*129.3*	*137.6*
U.K. Total (excl. Finance)	*44*	*100.0*	*79.0*	*115.9*	*123.1*	*114.9*
Rlys. and Transport O.U.K.	63 ⎫	100.0	31.9	31.8	38.1	31.1
Cables, Telegraphs	⎭	100.0	24.9	38.9	37.6	31.3
Mineral Properties	82 ⎱	100.0	57.4	166.5	215.6	188.2
Oil Concessions	⎰	100.0	86.8	122.2	177.2	136.9
Public Utilities	⁴	100.0	91.4	56.8	68.5	49.4
Land and Mortgage Concerns	⁴	100.0	53.7	67.0	65.2	56.2
Plantations	32	100.0	10.0	57.9	82.2	54.5
Banks	92	100.0	35.6	95.3	82.5	65.8
Other Concerns	47⁴,⁵	100.0	74.4	126.7	141.9	144.7
ADVENTURES O.U.K.	*59*	*100.0*	*45.3*	*82.2*	*102.6*	*86.6*
British Banks	⎫	100.0	22.7	−62.7	−73.3	−64.3
Foreign Banks in U.K.	40 ⎬	100.0	112.4	132.0	99.0	62.5
Insurance	⎭	100.0	114.4	131.3	121.2	117.3
Stockbrokers, Jobbers	61	100.0	79.6	102.2	22.9	1.1
Finance Companies, Bill-brokers	87 ⎬	100.0	86.7	103.4	46.4	24.6
Other Brokers and Agents	⎭	100.0	102.1	43.1	105.4	41.3
FINANCE	*59*	*100.0*	*72.6*	*51.1*	*25.2*	*10.4*
GRAND TOTAL	47	100.0	75.0	108.0	114.4	105.0

For 1909:
¹ Sugar and Glucose included in Brewing, etc.
² Furniture included in Building.
³ Public Amusements included in Misc. profits n.e.s.
⁴ Public Utilities and Land, etc., included in Other Concerns O.U.K.
⁵ Estimated on the basis of the gross *assessment* in 1911–12.

TABLE XIII

Index Numbers of Number of Assessments.[1] *All Enterprises*

	1909 (1911–12)	1927 (1928–29)	1932 (1933–34)	1936 (1937–38)	1937 (1938–39)	1938 (1939–40)
Coal Mines ..	.. 88.3	100.0	76.3	58.5	62.2	57.9
Iron Mines	.. 111	100	71	80	104	80.0
Other Mines ..	.. 169.6	100.0	87.6	96.9	81.4	69.6
Quarries ..	.. 131.1	100.0	93.1	76.9	74.5	73.3
EXTRACTION ..	.. *118.2*	*100.0*	*87.2*	*71.6*	*71.1*	*68.3*
Cotton	.. 95.1	100.0	59.8	67.9	65.0	57.8
Wool	.. 86.5	100.0	84.0	89.6	80.8	69.6
Silk	.. 36.9	100.0	100.2	99.4	107.2	85.1
Flax, Jute, Hemp ..	.. 87.9	100.0	76.2	99.6	74.2	83.5
Lace	.. 131.6	100.0	84.6	87.7	81.3	61.3
Hosiery ..	.. 32.8	100.0	95.4	86.1	79.0	88.4
Misc. Textiles ..	.. 86.0	100.0	92.4	103.0	94.5	83.9
Bleaching and Dyeing ..	.. 85.5	100.0	80.0	73.6	71.2	66.5
TEXTILES ..	.. *82.0*	*100.0*	*79.6*	*85.0*	*77.3*	*71.9*
Iron and Steel ..	.. 79.0	100.0	80.6	104.8	100.2	102.3
Machinery & Engineering	41.1	100.0	92.2	99.3	101.4	95.9
Shipbuilding ..	.. 37.2	100.0	88.7	96.2	98.6	91.8
Combines of above ..	49	100	159	200	173	173
Rly. Carriage and Wagon ..	58.6	100.0	80.0	75.7	54.2	82.9
Motor and Cycle	.. 32.7	100.0	88.6	86.4	81.6	86.6
Anchor, Chain, etc. ..	.. 62.3	100.0	74.9	100.4	86.8	81.6
Small Arms, Tools, etc. ..	44.7	100.0	81.2	79.4	71.0	85.5
Wrought Iron & Steel Tube	55.3	100.0	86.2	104.0	109.2	98.5
Copper and Brass ..	59.0	100.0	80.2	81.9	88.5	75.1
Gold and Silver Plate ..	64.3	100.0	88.9	83.5	76.3	71.5
Lead, Tin, Zinc ..	82.8	100.0	103.3	97.1	97.1	92.6
Tinplate.. ..	.. 24.0	100.0	86.6	82.3	80.3	78.3
Misc. Metals ..	.. 58.8	100.0	85.7	108.9	94.9	87.6
METALS ..	.. *48.9*	*100.0*	*87.6*	*94.1*	*92.4*	*90.2*
Grain Milling ..	.. 73.5	100.0	94.1	96.5	77.4	69.0
Biscuit & Bread (Wholesale)	33.2	100.0	111.1	109.9	108.1	132.9
Sugar and Glucose ..	22.7	100.0	91.6	146.3	108.4	115.8
Cocoa and Confectionery ..	59.9	100.0	97.9	97.8	77.1	86.1
Misc. Foods ..	.. 65.4	100.0	103.2	106.5	94.5	92.7
Brewing		100.0	87.2	77.0	79.6	79.0
Distilling ..	.. 105.3	100.0	62.4	83.8	100.9	79.5
Mineral Waters, etc. ..		100.0	76.6	50.8	50.2	46.8
Tobacco	95.0	100.0	112.5	99.2	99.6	90.8
FOOD, DRINK AND TOBACCO	*78.7*	*100.0*	*93.6*	*90.8*	*81.1*	*79.8*
Fine Chemicals	61.0	100.0	103.5	113.0	108.9	116.4
Patent Medicines ..	89.5	100.0	102.2	117.7	106.1	91.2
Soap and Candles ..	74.9	100.0	109.2	68.3	83.0	85.2
Fertilizers, Explosives, etc.	76.3	100.0	95.7	94.5	95.3	86.9
CHEMICALS ..	.. *71.5*	*100.0*	*99.7*	*100.2*	*99.6*	*97.3*

	1909 (1911–12)	1927 (1928–29)	1932 (1933–34)	1936 (1937–38)	1937 (1938–39)	1938 (1939–40)
Leather and Rubber ..	*67.8	100.0	81.3	84.1	75.3	69.7
Boots and Shoes ..	41.3	100.0	81.5	68.1	48.4	48.2
Misc. Clothing ..	41.6	100.0	91.6	84.3	75.9	70.8
Paper-making ..	56.2	100.0	103.2	110.9	116.5	100.2
Printing, Bookbinding ..	51.1	100.0	97.8	99.1	89.6	90.9
Publishing, Newspapers ..	81.2	100.0	92.3	105.7	104.7	101.5
Stationery ..	47.9	100.0	89.4	104.7	107.3	96.3
Furniture ..	[2]	100.0	85.9	70.0	63.9	63.3
Pottery, China, etc. ..	69.4	100.0	63.1	76.7	89.2	79.0
Glass	87.7	100.0	92.5	98.8	103.6	107.2
Instruments ..	45.4	100.0	96.7	93.9	77.5	113.2
Manufactures n.e.s. ..	58.9	100.0	90.0	88.6	85.0	80.5
OTHER MANUFACTURING ..	46.7[2]	100.0	91.0	88.7	80.6	81.2
Building & Contracting ..	54.7	100.0	102.6	108.8	103.2	95.9
Bricks, Cement, etc. ..	86.4	100.0	93.9	101.0	95.7	86.2
Timber ..	86.7[2]	100.0	93.2	96.0	80.2	77.3
BUILDING ..	64.6[2]	100.0	99.7	105.3	97.4	90.9
Gas	108.5	100.0	89.0	75.1	70.7	75.0
Water	129.0	100.0	99.7	86.3	81.4	76.8
Electricity ..	47.2	100.0	101.2	90.9	89.9	77.9
PUBLIC UTILITIES ..	103.9	100.0	96.6	83.7	79.8	76.4
MANUFACTURING INDUSTRY	59.8	100.0	92.2	93.8	87.4	84.9
Wholesale Distribution ..	53.4	100.0	92.7	90.1	84.0	81.4
Hotels, Inns, etc. ..	58.3	100.0	96.5	93.5	76.9	75.6
Retail (purely distributive)	27.7	100.0	108.5	106.2	103.6	101.6
Retail (semi-industrial) ..	19.5	100.0	108.9	108.1	101.9	99.5
DISTRIBUTION ..	30.5	100.0	105.9	104.0	98.2	96.1
Docks, Canals ..	108.9	100.0	97.3	84.7	74.4	75.4
Shipping ..	171.2	100.0	72.8	86.1	84.9	82.3
Ships' managers ..	124.8	100.0	69.1	63.2	58.4	60.3
Railways ..	153.6	100.0	92.9	33.0	29.5	31.2
Road Transport ..	13.8	100.0	115.1	117.6	99.5	113.1
Telephones ..	67	100	148	167	190	195
TRANSPORT ..	26.5	100.0	111.6	114.2	97.4	109.7
Law	104.8	100.0	98.3	99.4	97.5	97.7
Medicine and Dentistry ..	72.0	100.0	104.2	102.8	100.6	99.5
Literature and Art ..	68.0	100.0	113.1	112.5	106.5	104.1
Music and Drama ..	57.6	100.0	118.2	117.0	112.7	100.8
Accountancy ..	44.0	100.0	108.8	123.0	117.3	123.5
Engineering, Architecture ..	78.8	100.0	96.4	99.0	95.7	92.8
Other Professions ..	63.7	100.0	112.9	110.3	102.4	101.7
PROFESSIONS ..	70.6	100.0	107.4	107.5	102.9	101.6
Public Amusements ..	32.6	100.0	99.2	91.2	92.2	91.3
Fishing and Trawling ..	55.2	100.0	80.5	80.0	59.5	58.7
Markets, Tolls, etc. ..	94.2	100.0	75.7	57.7	48.0	42.0
Misc. profits n.e.s. ..	36.1	100.0	108.5	98.5	91.6	91.3
MISC. PROFITS ..	39.3	100.0	105.2	95.3	88.5	87.8
U.K. Total (excl. Finance) ..	38.8	100.0	104.6	102.7	96.5	95.0

	1909 (1911–12)	1927 (1928–29)	1932 (1933–34)	1936 (1937–38)	1937 (1938–39)	1938 (1939–40)
Rlys. and Transport O.U.K.	203.0	100.0	61.9	57.9	49.0	51.5
Cables, Telegraphs ..	58	100	41	34	34	15
Mineral Properties ..	186.1	100.0	80.0	79.7	89.1	70.0
Oil Concessions	88	100	77	73	59	40
Public Utilities	82	100	121	76	65	77
Land and Mortgage Concerns	71.1	100.0	93.4	57.1	61.9	44.0
Plantations ..	77.9	100.0	40.7	94.5	94.5	85.3
Banks	171	100	111	120	57	111
Other Concerns ..	66.2	100.0	97.1	77.7	75.2	75.3
ADVENTURES O.U.K. ..	*91.5*	*100.0*	*72.9*	*80.1*	*78.8*	*72.6*
British Banks ..	92.3 ⎫	100.0	93.9	97.0	98.2	86.1
Foreign Banks in U.K. ..	⎭	100	103	100	77	77
Insurance	20.0	100.0	114.9	101.4	96.0	100.4
Stockbrokers and Jobbers ..	120.6	100.0	91.1	90.5	68.7	69.0
Finance Companies, Bill-brokers ..	87.8	100.0	86.2	90.7	80.4	75.1
Other Brokers and Agents	86.9	100.0	102.2	93.5	79.8	82.0
FINANCE	*75.7*	*100.0*	*101.2*	*94.5*	*82.4*	*83.6*
GRAND TOTAL	*39.9*	*100.0*	*104.5*	*102.4*	*96.1*	*94.7*

[1] For trade groups in which the number of assessments in the base year, 1927, is less than 100, the index numbers are rounded to the nearest integer.

[2] Furniture inclided in Timber for 1909.

TABLE XIV

Percentage Distribution of Total Gross True Income by Trade Groups
All Enterprises in U.K. excluding Finance

	1909 (1911–12)	1927 (1928–29)	1932 (1933–34)	1936 (1937–38)	1937 (1938–39)	1938 (1939–40)
Coal Mines	4.6	1.5	1.9	2.2	2.2	2.4
Iron Mines	0.3 ⎫	0.1	..	..	0.1	0.1
Other Mines	⎬	0.1	..	0.1	0.1	..
Quarries	0.3 ⎭	0.4	0.3	0.4	0.5	0.4
EXTRACTION ..	*5.2*	*2.0*	*2.3*	*2.7*	*2.8*	*3.0*
Cotton	2.3	1.4	0.5	0.7	0.9	0.7
Wool	1.5	1.1	0.7	1.1	0.7	0.5
Silk	⎫	0.7	0.3	0.5	0.4	0.2
Flax, Jute, Hemp ..	⎪	0.3	0.1	0.2	0.2	0.1
Lace	1.6 ⎬	0.1	..	0.1	..	..
Hosiery	⎪	0.4	0.3	0.3	0.3	0.3
Misc. Textiles	⎭	0.1	0.1	0.1	0.1	0.1
Bleaching and Dyeing ..	0.7	0.5	0.3	0.2	0.2	0.1
TEXTILES	*6.1*	*4.5*	*2.5*	*3.2*	*3.0*	*2.1*

	1909 (1911–12)	1927 (1928–29)	1932 (1933–34)	1936 (1937–38)	1937 (1938–39)	1938 (1939–40)
Iron and Steel		0.6	0.5	1.2	1.8	1.7
Machinery and Engineering	5.7	3.2	2.3	4.4	5.5	6.4
Shipbuilding		0.2	0.1	0.3	0.3	0.7
Combines of above ..		0.2	0.2	0.6	0.8	1.0
Rly. Carriage and Wagon ..		0.1	0.1	0.1	0.2	0.2
Motor and Cycle		1.1	0.8	1.7	1.8	1.8
Anchor, Chain, etc. ..		0.1	0.1	0.2	0.2	0.2
Small Arms, Tools, etc. ..		0.4	0.4	0.7	0.7	0.9
Wrought Iron & Steel Tube	2.7	0.7	0.5	1.0	1.3	1.3
Copper and Brass ..		0.3	0.2	0.5	0.5	0.4
Gold and Silver Plate ..		0.2	0.2	0.2	0.2	0.2
Lead, Tin, Zinc ..		0.2	0.3	0.4	0.5	0.5
Tinplate..		0.1	0.1	0.2	0.2	0.1
Misc. Metals		0.1	0.1	0.3	0.3	0.2
METALS	8.4	7.4	5.7	11.9	14.4	15.5
Grain Milling		0.3	0.6	0.5	0.5	0.4
Biscuit & Bread (Wholesale)		0.4	0.4	0.2	0.2	0.2
Sugar and Glucose ..	2.1[1]	0.4	0.3	0.4	0.3	0.3
Cocoa and Confectionery ..		0.4	0.5	0.4	0.3	0.4
Misc. Foods		0.9	1.1	1.7	1.4	1.3
Brewing		3.0	2.8	2.6	2.4	2.7
Distilling	4.6[1]	0.6	0.5	0.6	0.6	0.6
Mineral Waters, etc. ..		0.2	0.2	0.2	0.1	0.1
Tobacco	0.8	1.5	1.5	1.5	1.5	1.6
FOOD, DRINK AND TOBACCO	7.4	7.7	8.0	8.1	7.3	7.7
Fine Chemicals		1.0	1.4	1.5	1.6	1.4
Patent Medicines ..	2.4	0.1	0.1	0.1	0.1	0.1
Soap and Candles ..		0.7	0.6	0.5	0.4	0.5
Fertilizers, Explosives, etc.		1.1	1.5	1.4	1.5	1.4
CHEMICALS	2.4.	2.9	3.6	3.5	3.6	3.5
Leather and Rubber ..		1.0	0.7	0.9	0.7	0.7
Boots and Shoes ..	2.1	0.5	0.3	0.3	0.2	0.2
Misc. Clothing ..		1.2	0.9	0.7	0.8	0.7
Paper-making		0.5	0.8	0.9	0.9	0.9
Printing, Bookbinding ..	2.6	0.9	0.8	0.8	0.8	0.8
Publishing, Newspapers ..		1.7	1.3	1.4	1.3	1.1
Stationery		0.3	0.3	0.4	0.5	0.5
Furniture	[2]	0.4	0.2	0.3	0.2	0.2
Pottery, China, etc. ..		0.2	0.1	0.2	0.1	0.2
Glass	1.0	0.2	0.2	0.4	0.3	0.4
Instruments		0.7	0.4	0.5	0.5	0.5
Manufactures n.e.s. ..		0.5	0.7	0.6	0.6	0.5
OTHER MANUFACTURING ..	5.8[2]	8.0	6.8	7.4	7.0	6.7
Building and Contracting ..		2.0	2.0	2.0	1.9	1.9
Bricks, Cement, etc. ..	2.5[2]	0.8	0.9	1.2	1.0	1.2
Timber		0.5	0.5	0.7	0.6	0.5
BUILDING	2.5[2]	3.3	3.3	3.9	3.5	3.6
Gas	2.3	1.8	2.2	1.4	1.3	1.4
Water	1.7	1.0	1.6	1.2	1.2	1.1
Electricity	1.1[5]	2.0	3.8	3.0	3.1	3.3
PUBLIC UTILITIES ..	5.0	4.8	7.6	5.6	5.6	5.8

	1909 (1911–12)	1927 (1928–29)	1932 (1933–34)	1936 (1937–38)	1937 (1938–39)	1938 (1939–40)
MANUFACTURING INDUSTRY	37.6	38.6	37.5	43.6	44.4	44.8
Wholesale Distribution ..	12.3	10.0	7.6	8.5	8.5	7.6
Hotels, Inns, etc. ..	⎫	3.5	2.7	2.5	2.2	2.2
Retail (purely distributive)	14.7 ⎬	13.0	14.5	12.2	11.5	11.4
Retail (semi-industrial) ..	⎭	10.3	10.9	8.7	7.6	7.8
DISTRIBUTION	27.0	36.9	35.7	31.9	29.8	29.0
Docks, Canals	1.1	0.7	0.9	0.6	0.6	0.6
Shipping	4.4[5] ⎫	2.8	1.4	2.4	3.7	3.2
Ships' managers	⎭	0.1	0.1	0.1	0.1	0.1
Railways	12.1	4.4	3.6	2.8	2.9	2.9
Road Transport	1.9[5]	2.7	3.8	3.7	3.9	4.0
Telephones	0.3[5]	..	..	..	..	..
TRANSPORT	19.8	10.7	9.8	9.6	11.2	10.9
Law	⎫	2.0	2.4	1.9	1.8	1.8
Medicine and Dentistry ..	⎪	2.9	3.6	3.0	2.9	3.1
Literature and Art ..	⎪	0.3	0.4	0.4	0.3	0.3
Music and Drama ..	8.3 ⎬	0.3	0.3	0.3	0.3	0.3
Accountancy	⎪	1.0	1.3	1.1	0.9	1.0
Engineering & Architecture	⎪	0.8	0.8	0.8	0.9	0.9
Other Professions ..	⎭	1.6	1.8	1.6	1.5	1.5
PROFESSIONS	8.3	8.9	10.5	9.1	8.6	8.8
Public Amusements ..	[3]	0.8	1.3	1.0	1.2	1.1
Fishing and Trawling ..	0.2[5]	0.2	0.1	0.2	0.2	0.1
Markets, Tolls, etc. ..	0.3	0.2	0.2	0.2	0.2	0.1
Misc. profits n.e.s. ..	1.5[3,5]	1.7	2.5	1.6	1.5	2.1
MISC. PROFITS	2.0	2.9	4.2	3.0	3.1	3.5
U.K. Total (excl. Finance) ..	100.0	100.0	100.0	100.0	100.0	100.0

For 1909:
[1] Sugar and Glucose included in Brewing, etc.
[2] Furniture included in Building.
[3] Public Amusements included in Misc. profits n.e.s.
[5] Estimated on the basis of the gross *assessment* in 1911–12.

TABLE XV

Percentage Distribution of Numbers of Assessments by Trade Groups
All Enterprises in U.K., excluding Finance

	1909 (1911–12)	1927 (1928–29)	1932 (1933–34)	1936 (1937–38)	1937 (1938–39)	1938 (1939–40)
Coal Mines	0.4	0.2	0.1	0.1	0.1	0.1
Iron Mines	..	..	..	..	..	..
Other Mines	0.1	..	..	..	..	..
Quarries	1.0	0.3	0.3	0.2	0.2	0.2
EXTRACTION	1.5	0.5	0.4	0.3	0.4	0.3

	1909 (1911–12)	1927 (1928–29)	1932 (1933–34)	1936 (1937–38)	1937 (1938–39)	1938 (1939–40)
Cotton	0.5	0.2	0.1	0.1	0.1	0.1
Wool	0.4	0.2	0.1	0.2	0.2	0.1
Silk	..	..	..	..	0.1	..
Flax, Jute, Hemp	0.2	0.1	0.1	0.1	0.1	0.1
Lace	0.2	..	..	..	..	..
Hosiery	0.1	0.1	0.1	0.1	0.1	0.1
Misc. Textiles	0.1	..	..	..	..	..
Bleaching and Dyeing	0.2	0.1	0.1	0.1	0.1	0.1
TEXTILES	1.7	0.8	0.6	0.7	0.6	0.6
Iron and Steel	0.3	0.2	0.1	0.2	0.2	0.2
Machinery and Engineering	0.8	0.8	0.7	0.8	0.8	0.8
Shipbuilding	0.1	0.1	0.1	0.1	0.1	0.1
Combines of above	..	..	..	..	..	..
Rly. Carriage and Wagon						
Motor and Cycle	0.2	0.2	0.2	0.2	0.2	0.2
Anchor, Chain, etc.	0.1	..	..	..	..	..
Small Arms, Tools, etc.	0.3	0.3	0.2	0.2	0.2	0.2
Wrought Iron & Steel Tube	0.3	0.2	0.2	0.2	0.2	0.2
Copper and Brass	0.2	0.1	0.1	0.1	0.1	0.1
Gold and Silver Plate	0.3	0.2	0.2	0.2	0.1	0.1
Lead, Tin, Zinc	0.1	..	..	..	..	..
Tinplate	..	..	..	..	..	..
Misc. Metals	0.1	0.1	0.1	0.1	0.1	0.1
METALS	2.8	2.2	1.8	2.0	2.1	2.1
Grain Milling	0.4	0.2	0.2	0.2	0.2	0.1
Biscuit & Bread (Wholesale)	..	..	..	..	..	0.1
Sugar and Glucose	..	..	..	..	..	..
Cocoa and Confectionery	0.1	0.1	0.1	0.1	0.1	0.1
Misc. Foods	0.3	0.2	0.2	0.2	0.2	0.2
Brewing	} 0.7	0.2	0.1	0.1	0.1	0.1
Distilling		..	..	..	..	..
Mineral Waters, etc.		0.1	0.1	0.1	0.1	0.1
Tobacco	0.1	..	..	..	..	..
FOOD, DRINK AND TOBACCO	1.6	0.8	0.7	0.7	0.7	0.7
Fine Chemicals	0.2	0.1	0.1	0.1	0.1	0.2
Patent Medicines	..	..	..	..	..	..
Soap and Candles	0.1	..	..	..	..	..
Fertilizers, Explosives, etc.	0.4	0.2	0.2	0.2	0.2	0.2
CHEMICALS	0.7	0.4	0.3	0.4	0.4	0.4
Leather and Rubber	0.5	0.3	0.2	0.2	0.2	0.2
Boots and Shoes	0.2	0.2	0.2	0.2	0.1	0.1
Misc. Clothing	0.9	0.8	0.7	0.7	0.6	0.6
Paper-making	0.1	0.1	0.1	0.1	0.1	0.1
Printing, Bookbinding	1.0	0.8	0.7	0.7	0.7	0.7
Publishing, Newspapers	0.4	0.2	0.2	0.2	0.2	0.2
Stationery	0.2	0.1	0.1	0.1	0.2	0.1
Furniture	[2]	0.3	0.3	0.2	0.2	0.2
Pottery, China, etc.	0.1	0.1	..	..	0.1	..
Glass	0.1	..	..	..	..	..
Instruments	0.4	0.3	0.3	0.3	0.3	0.4
Manufactures n.e.s.	0.2	0.2	0.1	0.1	0.1	0.1
OTHER MANUFACTURING	4.0[2]	3.3	2.9	2.9	2.8	2.8

	1909 (1911–12)	1927 (1928–29)	1932 (1933–34)	1936 (1937–38)	1937 (1938–39)	1938 (1939–40)
Building and Contracting ..	2.3	1.7	1.6	1.7	1.8	1.7
Bricks, Cement, etc. ..	0.5	0.2	0.2	0.2	0.2	0.2
Timber	1.2[2]	0.5	0.5	0.5	0.4	0.4
BUILDING	4.0[2]	2.4	2.3	2.5	2.4	2.3
Gas	0.4	0.1	0.1	0.1	0.1	0.1
Water	0.7	0.2	0.2	0.2	0.2	0.2
Electricity	0.1	0.1	0.1	0.1	0.1	0.1
PUBLIC UTILITIES ..	1.2	0.4	0.4	0.4	0.4	0.4
MANUFACTURING INDUSTRY	15.9	10.3	9.1	9.4	9.3	9.2
Wholesale Distribution ..	7.8	5.7	5.0	5.0	4.9	4.9
Hotels, Inns, etc. ..	11.6	7.7	7.1	7.0	6.1	6.1
Retail (purely distributive)	20.6	28.9	29.9	29.9	31.0	30.9
Retail (semi-industrial) ..	11.9	23.8	24.7	25.0	25.1	24.9
DISTRIBUTION	51.9	66.0	66.8	66.9	67.2	66.8
Docks, Canals	0.1	..	..	..	..	..
Shipping	0.8	0.2	0.1	0.2	0.2	0.2
Ships' managers	0.2	0.1	..	..	..	..
Railways	..	..	..	..	..	..
Road Transport	1.0	2.9	3.2	3.4	3.0	3.5
Telephones	..	..	..	..	..	..
TRANSPORT	2.2	3.2	3.4	3.6	3.3	3.7
Law	3.5	1.2	1.2	1.2	1.2	1.3
Medicine and Dentistry ..	5.6	3.0	3.0	3.0	3.1	3.1
Literature and Art ..	1.3	0.8	0.8	0.8	0.8	0.8
Music and Drama ..	1.1	0.8	0.9	0.9	0.9	0.8
Accountancy	0.9	0.8	0.8	0.9	0.9	1.0
Engineering, Architecture ..	1.7	0.8	0.8	0.8	0.8	0.8
Other Professions ..	5.0	3.1	3.3	3.3	3.2	3.3
PROFESSIONS	18.9	10.4	10.7	10.9	11.1	11.1
Public Amusements ..	0.7	0.8	0.8	0.7	0.8	0.8
Fishing and Trawling ..	0.4	0.3	0.2	0.2	0.2	0.2
Markets, Tolls, etc. ..	1.1	0.5	0.3	0.3	0.2	0.2
Misc. profits n.e.s. ..	7.4	8.0	8.3	7.6	7.6	7.7
MISC. PROFITS	9.7	9.6	9.6	8.9	8.8	8.9
U.K. Total (excl. Finance) ..	100.0	100.0	100.0	100.0	100.0	100.0

[2] Furniture included in Timber for 1909.

APPENDIX A

THE TRADE CLASSIFICATION

The following is a descriptive list of the trade groups used in this report. The trade groups are arranged in the same order as in the Main Tables.

EXTRACTION
1. Coal Mines
2. Iron Mines
3. Mines—other than coal and iron
4. Quarries

TEXTILES
1. Cotton—spinning, weaving, etc.
2. Wool and Worsted—spinning, weaving, alpaca, mohair, carpets, etc.
3. Silk—throwing, spinning, weaving, ribbons, etc.
4. Flax, Jute and Hemp—scutching, linens; rope, twine and net; sacks, bags, sails, canvas, tarpaulins, etc.
5. Lace—including muslin curtains, etc.
6. Hosiery—machine-knitted articles
7. Miscellaneous—e.g. elastic webbing; cocoanut fibre, horsehair, feathers (not ornamental), and sundry vegetable fibres; flock and rag; velvet and fustian cutting
8. Bleaching, Dyeing, Printing and Finishing—for textiles generally wherever separate.

METALS
1. Ironworks; Iron and Steel—casting, founding, forging, rolling, smelting; bars, ingots, plates and sheets, etc.; scrap
2. Machinery and Mechanical Engineering Trades—including electrical engineering, but not including civil engineering contracting
3. Shipbuilding and Marine Engineering
4. Iron and Steel Concerns—large combinations of the above three classes
5. Railway Carriage, Wagon, and Tramcar Building

6. Cycle and Motor Trades
7. Anchor, Chain, Nail, Bolt, Rivet and Screw Trade
8. Small Arms, Cutlery, Tools, Implements; Needle, Pin, Fish-hook and Button Trade; Locks, Safes
9. Wrought Iron and Steel Tubes, Wire Trade, Galvanized Sheet, Hardware, Hollow-Ware, Tinned and Japanned Goods and Bedsteads
10. Copper and Brass Trades—smelting, rolling, casting and finished trades
11. Gold and Silver Plate and Plated Goods, Watches, Clocks and Jewellery
12. Lead, Tin, Zinc and other metals
13. Tinplate Trade.
14. Miscellaneous Metal Industries—e.g. art metal goods, air-tight coffins, meters, metal pulpits, etc.

FOOD, DRINK AND TOBACCO
1. Grain Milling
2. Biscuit and Bread Making (Wholesale)
3. Sugar and Glucose
4. Cocoa, Confectionery, and Fruit Preserving
5. Miscellaneous Food Trades—e.g. preserved meats, fish curing, pickles, sauces; bacon curing; butter, cheese, margarine; animal foods; salt; other food preparations
6. Brewing—including bottlers and malsters.
7. Distilling—rectifying, compounding, methylating
8. Mineral Waters—including cider and wines
9. Tobacco

CHEMICALS
1. Fine Chemicals—including coal tar products, drugs and perfumery
2. Patent Medicines
3. Soap and Candle Trades
4. Fertilizers and Explosives—seed crushing; oil and tallow, glue, disinfectants; paint, colour and varnish; ammunition, fire-works; matches and firelighters, household polishing articles

OTHER MANUFACTURING
1. Leather and India-rubber—fellmongery, tanning, dressing, miscellaneous leather and rubber goods, saddlery, etc.

K

2. Boots and Shoes
3. Miscellaneous Clothing Trades—ready-made clothes; hats, furs, millinery, umbrellas, artificial flowers and ornamental feathers, cleaning and dyeing.
4. Paper-making
5. Printing, Bookbinding, Typefounding, Stereotyping, Engraving and Die-sinking
6. Newspapers and other Periodicals, and Publishing Trades
7. Miscellaneous Stationery Trades—e.g. ink, notepaper, pens, pencils, cardboard boxes, etc.
8. Furniture, Cabinet Making, and Upholstery
9. Pottery, China and Earthenware
10. Glass and Glass Articles
11. Instruments, Musical, Scientific and Sporting—including toys, fancy articles, photographic requisities, etc.
12. Miscellaneous Manufacturing and Productive Industries, not included above

BUILDING
1. Building and Works Contracting—including civil engineering work, public and private
2. Bricks and Cement—including other building accessories
3. Timber and Allied Trades—excluding furniture, etc.

PUBLIC UTILITIES
1. Gasworks
2. Waterworks
3. Electric Power and Light.

Manufacturing Industry. All the above industries, excepting Extraction.

DISTRIBUTION
1. Wholesale—merchants, warehousemen, agents, etc., distributing merchandise but not working upon it other than by sorting or blending
2. Hotels, Inns—including all retailers of wines, spirits, beer and liquors

3. Retail, purely distributive
4. Retail, semi-industrial—i.e. having manufacturing and productive elements, e.g. carpenter, laundry, baker, tailor

TRANSPORT
1. Docks, Canals, Bridges, Ferries, Navigable Waters
2. Shipping
2A Ships' managers
3. Railways
4. Tramways, Omnibuses, Carriers, Motor and Cab Proprietors, Removers, etc.
5. Telephones

PROFESSIONS
1. Law
2. Medicine and Dentistry
3. Literature and Art
4. Music and Drama
5. Accountancy
6. Engineering, Land Surveying and Architecture
7. All Other Professions

MISCELLANEOUS
1. Public Amusements—theatres, cinemas, football clubs, etc.
2. Fishing and Trawling
3. Minor Concerns—markets, tolls, fishings, cemeteries and salt springs
4. Miscellaneous Profits (not elsewhere specified)

ADVENTURES OUTSIDE U.K.
1. Railways, Tramways, etc.
2. Cables, Telegraphs and Telephones
3. Mineral Properties
4. Oil Companies
5. Gasworks and Waterworks
6. Land and Mortgage Companies
7. Plantations—of tea, coffee, sugar, rubber, etc.
8. U.K. Banks—carrying on business mainly out of the U.K.
9. Other Profits from Abroad (not elsewhere specified)

K.I

FINANCE

1. U.K. Banks—carrying on business mainly in the U.K.
2. Foreign Banks—profits of U.K. branches
3. Insurance
4. Stock and Share Brokers and Jobbers
5. Finance Companies and Agencies, Bill and Discount Brokers, etc.
6. All other Brokers and Agents (not classed under distribution)—including some non-financial agencies, e.g. for advertising, tourism, entertainment, housing, etc.

APPENDIX B

ANALYSIS ACCORDING TO YEAR OF ASSESSMENT OF SCHEDULE D ASSESSMENTS MADE IN EACH YEAR 1926–27 TO 1939–40

Year in which assessed		Percentage of assessment in respect of:			Total gross assessment £mn.
		Current year	Previous year	Earlier years	
1926–27	.. ..	92.3	7.7		1,189
1927–28	.. ..	92.6	7.4		1,160
1928–29	.. ..	93.3	2.9	3.8	1,212
1929–30	.. ..	92.3	3.4	4.3	1,241
1930–31	.. ..	N.A.	N.A.	N.A.	N.A.
1931–32	.. ..	92.4	3.4	4.2	1,095
1932–33	.. ..	92.3	3.4	4.3	977
1933–34	.. ..	92.5	3.6	4.0	943
1934–35	.. ..	91.8	3.8	4.5	998
1935–36	.. ..	N.A.	N.A.	N.A.	N.A.
1936–37	.. ..	93.8	3.3	2.9	1,120
1937–38	.. ..	93.6	3.5	3.0	1,247
1938–39	.. ..	94.2	3.0	2.7	1,285
1939–40	.. ..	94.0	3.6	2.6	1,207

NOTE.—Deductions for wear and tear, losses and personal allowances were extracted for assessments for the current year but not for previous years. The total gross assessments shown in the last column therefore differ from the figures published in the Board's annual reports. Also, the percentage breakdown shown in this table will slightly understate the proportion attributable to the current year.

APPENDIX C
Schedule D Assessments, 1928–29 to 1939–40

£ million	1928–9	1929–30	1930–1	1931–2	1932–3	1933–4	1934–5	1935–6	1936–7	1937–8	1938–9	1939–40
Manufacturing, Productive and Mining Industries ..	478	478	476	429	350	332	367	390	426	485	586	545
Distribution, Transport and Communication ..	524	531	538	483	418	391	416	427	465	505	523	493
Finance, Professions and other Profits	198	212	192	174	176	177	184	187	195	217	203	186
Total Gross Assessments of the above	1,200	1,222	1,207	1,086	944	900	967	1,004	1,086	1,207	1,312	1,224
Wear and Tear Allowances	80	88	93	87	89	96	100	112	122	136	171	175
Other Reductions and Discharges	221	224	246	229	209	187	186	187	184	217	225	195
Total Net Assessments ..	899	910	867	769	646	617	682	705	780	853	915	854
Indices of Assessment ..												
Manufacturing, etc. ..	100.0	100.0	99.7	89.7	73.2	69.5	76.8	81.6	89.2	101.5	122.7	114.0
Distribution, Transport ..	100.0	101.5	102.8	92.2	79.8	74.7	79.5	81.6	88.8	96.4	99.8	94.2
Finance, Professions, etc. ..	100.0	107.2	96.8	87.8	88.7	89.2	92.8	94.2	98.3	109.4	102.3	94.1
Gross Assessment ..	100.0	101.9	100.6	90.5	78.7	75.0	80.6	83.7	90.5	100.6	109.3	102.0
Net Assessment ..	100.0	101.3	96.5	85.5	71.9	68.6	75.8	78.4	86.8	94.9	101.8	95.0

Source: Inland Revenue Reports.

NOTE. The classification of gross assessments used in this table is taken from the Inland Revenue reports. It does not exhaust the whole of the gross assessments, which also include income from interest earned in the U.K. and overseas. The deductions made against the gross assessment to arrive at the 'net assessment' figures refer to *all* Schedule D income, so that the net assessments shown in the Table are smaller than the true amounts for the trading activities which have been classified here.

COMMENT. The index numbers for gross assessment in the last three years do not at first sight appear to correspond very closely with the index numbers for Gross True Income, although they are identical for the assessment year 1933–4 (1932). (See Main Table XII—Grand Total). This is partly due to the special nature of the figures for Finance. (See Appendix to Chapter III). By excluding the gross assessment for the finance group (U.K.) from the total in this table, and by deducting the Gross True Income of Finance from the grand total of Gross True Income, we get the following figures.

	1928–9	1933–4	1938–9
Gross assessment £m.	1,119	838	1,246
Indices of gross assessment	100.0	74.9	111.3
Gross True Income £m.	947	712	1,144
Indices of Gross True Income	100.0	75.2	120.8

Comparable figures for 1937–8 and 1939–40 cannot be given, as figures for the gross assessments of Finance are not available.

The two indices for 1933–4 are approximately equal, but there is a wide divergence for 1938–9. If 'profits' were measured by the gross assessments, the percentage increase over the ten year period would be little more than one half that obtained by using the Gross True Income figures. It does not appear, therefore, that the figures of gross assessment could be used to provide reliable estimates of Gross True Income for the intervening years of our series in the Main Tables. Furthermore, what applies to the whole applies even more to the parts. The gross assessments for manufacturing, etc., move in a manner which is even more out of line with the trend shown by the comparable Gross True Income figures.

APPENDIX D

Profits Assessed in 1890–1 and 1895–6

Trade classifications of trading profits assessed under Schedule D in 1890–1 and 1895–6 were made by the Inland Revenue authorities at the time. Little is known of the way in which the classification was made and there is some uncertainty as to the exact income concept on which the tabulation is based. The results of these early trade classifications are probably not strictly comparable with each other, or with the classification for 1911–12. At the same time they have some historical interest and are reproduced in the following tables.

The classifications for 1890–1 and 1895–6 appear to be tabulations of a quantity analogous to 'Actual Income' (described as 'Net Profit charged to Duty') rather than of 'True Income' as defined in the main body of this report. The income classified in 1890–1 and 1895–6 presumably excludes all profits below the current exemption limit (£150 in 1890–1 and £160 in 1895–6) and about £5 million of 'unassessed' duty under Schedule D. The income classified in 1890–91 and 1895–96 was certainly net of Wear and Tear allowances. In that sense it corresponds more closely with Net True Income than with Gross True Income. The total amount of income classified fell short of the amount of Net True Income (as far as that quantity can be satisfactorily estimated) by some £15 m. in 1890–91 and £18 m. in 1895–96. However, the total Net True Income for these years is not exactly known. Wear and Tear allowances amounted to about £4.3 m. in 1890–91 and £4.9 m. in 1895–96. These totals were not divided among the various trade groups, so it is impossible to estimate the Gross True Income of these groups.

The assessments made in 1890–91 and 1895–96 were generally based on averages of taxable profits over numbers of preceding years, and do not refer to any single accounting year. Mines were assessed over a five-year average; railways, gasworks, quarries, some ironworks, waterworks, canals, docks and harbours, markets, tolls, etc., were assessed on the profits of the preceding year (in the present examples, 1889–90 and 1894–95); all other concerns were assessed on a three-year average. (This is the same method as was used in 1911–12).

The basis of the trade classification used in 1890–91 and 1895–96 has not been preserved. It seems likely that the basis changed between the two years. The apparent decline from 148,000 to 110,000 in the number of assessments made on retail traders, and the increase from 36,000 to 66,000 in the number of assessments on 'miscellaneous profits not elsewhere specified' were pointed out some years later by Departmental statisticians as signs of a change in the basis of classification between 1890–91 and 1895–96. This would mean that the results of the two tabulations would not be strictly comparable with each other.

It does not follow, however, that all the trade groups were affected to the same extent. The sub-totals for some of the major industrial groups ('textile trades' and public utilities in particular), and the figures for some important separate trade groups (such as cotton, brewing and distilling, and railways) probably reflect fairly accurate and unchanging classifications of the original returns. The amounts of income for each of these trades shown for the two years 1890–91 and 1895–96 are therefore probably comparable with each other, except in so far as they were affected by the change in the exemption limit between the two assessments. In the same way, the figures shown for these early years for some major trade groups may be comparable with those shown in the main tables for 1911–12. This is probably true of the examples already given (cotton, brewing and distilling, and railways). It is likely to be less true of many other trade groups, and even of the industrial sub-totals. The uncertainty concerning the whole distributive group has been mentioned already. It must be remembered that the productive sector of the economy was divided into some 50 trade groups in 1890–91 and 1895–96, and into 90 trade groups in 1911–12.[1] Moreover, while the exemption limit remained unchanged between 1895–96 and 1911–12, the scope of the assessments probably increased as a result of improvements of administration. In effect, therefore, the figures for 1890–91 and 1895–96 probably represented a smaller proportion of the taxable income actually accruing in the corresponding accounting periods than the figures for 1911–12 did.

The total amount of trading income classified in the tables was about £262 m. in 1890–91 and about £256 m. in 1895–96. These figures represent almost the whole of the trading profits net of Wear and Tear, as defined for Income Tax purposes, from all productive activity.

[1] Though some of these had to be recombined to form trade groups in the main tables of this report.

Some £15–20 m. should probably be added to make these totals correspond with the 'Net True Income' for these years. The totals exclude interest and the profits of agriculture, and most of the profits accruing in sums below the exemption limit. They include, however, £20 m. in 1890–91 and £27 m. in 1895–96, representing identifiable income from abroad. The total classified income from productive activity inside the United Kingdom amounted to about £242 m. in 1890–91 and £229 m. in 1895–96. These sums presumably fell short of the 'Net True Income' of those assessment years by some £13–18 m.

The total number of assessments made, which may be interpreted as a rough indication of the number of concerns assessed, was about 391,600 in 1890–91 and 373,000 in 1895–96. Of these assessments, about 389,000 and 371,000 respectively were made on concerns operating mainly inside the United Kingdom. It may, however, be assumed that there existed a fairly large number of small concerns which were not assessed to Income Tax, though their combined taxable income was probably not proportionately great. The average income per assessment on concerns operating inside the United Kingdom was about £620 in both years.

Assessments to Income Tax under Schedule D in certain trade groups, 1890–91 and 1895–96.

					Net Profits £000		Number of assessments	
					1890–1	*1895–6*	*1890–1*	*1895–6*
1.	Coal Mines	..	..	..	7,350	11,370	1,691	1,630
2.	Other Mines	..	..	..	1,170	650	443	346
3.	Quarries	..	..	..	890	1,090	3,584	3,852
4.	Salt Springs	..	..	..	390	200	23	29
Extraction		..	..	..	*9,800*	*13,310*	*5,741*	*5,857*
5.	Cotton	..	..	..	4,300	4,530	2,548	2,320
6.	Wool	..	..	..	3,940	3,320	2,243	2,032
7.	Silk	..	..	..	490	250	304	278
8.	Flax, Jute, Hemp	..	..	..	1,660	1,140	1,225	893
9.	Ready-made Clothing	..	..	..	1,120	970	1,600	1,294
10.	Misc. Textiles	..	..	..	1,040	800	1,232	1,387
Textiles		..	..	..	*12,550*	*11,000*	*9,152*	*8,204*
11.	Iron and Steel	..	..	..	10,800	8,090	4,152	3,888
12.	Brass, Copper and Lead	..	..	..	2,200	780	1,080	863
13.	Hardware	..	..	..	1,120	1,070	1,654	1,135
14.	Gold and Silver	..	..	..	700	1,010	1,523	1,232
15.	Misc. Metal trades	..	..	..	730	1,420	884	1,339
Metals		..	..	..	*15,560*	*12,370*	*9,293*	*8,457*

			Net Profits £000		Number of assessments	
			1890-1	1895-6	1890-1	1895-6
16.	Shipbuilding	..	770	700	335	332
17.	Carriage and Wagon building	..	630	750	1,298	1,376
18.	Sugar Refining	..	450	340	42	30
19.	Brewing, Distilling ..	..	11,690	12,680	3,681	3,414
20.	Paper-making	..	1,000	940	363	320
21.	Tanning	..	570	590	540	451
22.	Leather, Indiarubber ..	..	1,470	1,740	2,813	2,749
23.	Glass, China	..	1,860	1,580	2,878	2,661
24.	Chemicals	..	4,340	4,390	2,006	1,815
	Miscellaneous	..	6,450	7,830	10,584	10,672
Other Manufacturing ..	..	..	*29,230*	*31,530*	*24,540*	*23,820*
25.	Gasworks	..	5,050	5,920	1,607	1,601
26.	Waterworks	..	3,540	3,940	1,050	1,388
Public Utilities ..	..	..	*8,590*	*9,860*	*2,657*	*2,989*
27.	Wholesale	..	29,160	26,610	25,692	25,876
28.	Hotels, Inns, etc.	..	8,480	7,830	51,010	45,372
29.	Retail	..	23,320	17,550	147,842	109,697
Distribution	..	..	*60,960*	*52,000*	*224,544*	*180,945*
30.	Docks, Canals, etc. ..	..	3,650	3,750	857	692
31.	Shipping	..	11,420	5,350	6,691	4,695
32.	Railways..	..	36,450	36,460	164	178
33.	Tramways, Omnibuses ..	..	1,450	1,530	2,332	2,103
Transport	..	..	*52,960*	*47,090*	*10,044*	*7,668*
34.	Banking	..	7,990	7,120	401	386
35.	Insurance	..	3,040	3,460	794	1,044
36.	Finance corporations,					
	Stock brokers	..	9,730	5,940	3,611	3,297
37.	Other brokers	..	2,230	1,880	6,869	6,104
Finance	..	..	*23,000*	*18,400*	*11,675*	*10,831*
	Law	..	7,590	7,500	12,421	12,494
	Medicine	..	4,920	5,030	15,205	16,967
	Other Professions ..	..	6,160	5,840	24,777	23,779
Professions (ex. Literature) ..	..	..	*18,670*	*18,360*	*52,403*	*53,240*
Literature, Publishing, etc. ..	..	2,890	2,970	2,709	3,013
Miscellaneous Profits n.e.s. ..	..	7,960	12,240	36,394	66,377
Total: Concerns in U.K.	..	*242,180*	*229,110*	*389,152*	*371,401*
	Railways O.U.K. ..	..	7,580	7,010	621	527
	Telegraphs	..	1,380	1,240	29	51
	Mines	..	2,090	5,150	295	246
	Gas, Waterworks	..	1,360	2,100	59	96
	Land, Mortgage	..	3,540	5,430	281	238
	Other Profits	..	3,920	5,920	595	695
Adventures O.U.K.[1] ..	..	*19,880*	*26,850*	*1,880*	*1,853*
GRAND TOTAL	..	..	*262,050*	*255,960*	*391,032*	*373,254*

[1] In so far as identifiable.

CLASSIFICATION OF CONCERNS, 1890–1 AND 1895–6

(5) Cotton: All branches, including spinning, weaving, etc.

(6) Wool: All branches, including spinning, weaving, etc.

(7) Silk: All branches including throwing, weaving, lace, ribbons, etc.

(8) Flax, Jute, Hemp: including linens, sacking, sails, cordage, cables, and ropes.

(9) Ready-made clothing: includes hosiery, hats, and caps (*not* boots and shoes).

(11) Iron and Steel: includes furnaces, foundries, mills, machinery and engineering.

(12) Brass, copper and lead: includes foundries, tin and tinplate.

(13) Hardware: includes cutlery, implements, guns, locks, screws and nails.

(14) Gold and silver: includes plate and plated goods, watches, clocks, jewellery.

(17) Carriage building: includes railway and other carriages, vans, carts, drays.

(19) Brewing, distilling: includes mineral waters.

(22) Leather, india rubber: includes boots and shoes and harness.

(23) Glass, china: includes earthenware, bricks, tiles, drainpipes, cement.

(24) Chemicals: includes oils, paints, varnish, soap, candles.

(27) Wholesale Distribution: includes merchants, warehousemen, brokers, agents, connected with distribution of goods, produce and merchandise.

(28) Hotels, Inns: includes taverns, beer houses, refreshment houses and all retailers of wines, spirits, beer and liquors.

(29) Retail Distribution: all retail traders not included in (28).

(30) Docks, canals: includes bridges, ferries, navigable waters, and tolls derived therefrom.

(33) Tramways, omnibuses: includes carriers.

(36) Finance corporations, stock brokers: includes agencies, bill-brokers and discount houses.

APPENDIX E

SELF-EMPLOYED PERSONS ASSESSED UNDER SCHEDULE D IN 1928–29

The number of assessments made in any given year provides a rough indication of the number of concerns operating in the corresponding accounting year. The main reasons why the indication is not exact have been discussed in the body of this report. They are (i) the fact that some concerns are assessed more than once in each assessment year, (ii) the fact that the assessments made in any assessment year include some assessments brought forward from earlier years and exclude some assessments carried forward for agreement in later years, (iii) the exclusion of enterprises with no profit, and (iv) the exclusion of some non-corporate enterprises with a profit below the exemption limit. In general, however, the number of assessments made in any given year probably provides a fairly close estimate of the number of concerns in any given trade group in the corresponding accounting year, except in those trades, like retail distribution, where there may be large numbers of enterprises below the exemption limit.

The total number of assessments can be divided between corporate and non–corporate enterprises as has been done in this report. For some purposes, however, it is necessary to know not the number of concerns, corporate or non-corporate, but the number of 'entrepreneurial persons' associated with these concerns. Complete information on this point is not available for any of the years covered by this report, but exact information about the non-corporate concerns is available for 1928–29 (1927).

The total number of self-employed 'entrepreneurial persons' covered by the Schedule D assessments consists of three groups:

  (i) individual traders,
  (ii) members of non-corporate partnerships,
  (iii) members of partnerships trading as 'private companies'.

The material at our disposal throws no light on the number of private companies assessed. The number of entrepreneurial persons trading in such companies is therefore unknown. It certainly tended to increase throughout the period 1910–1940.

The number of assessments made on individuals in 1928–29 and the number of members of non-corporate partnerships assessed in that year are known, and by adding the two the numbers of 'entrepreneurial persons' trading in non-corporate enterprises in 1928–29 can be estimated. The results are shown in Table E. These totals somewhat overstate the number of 'self-employed persons' trading in any given year, because any trader engaged in more than one branch of activity might, if he wished, be assessed separately in respect of each activity.

It will be seen from Table E that the total number of 'entrepreneurial persons' associated with the non-corporate concerns assessed for the U.K. in 1928–29 was 1,064,304. Of these, 814,713 or 76.5 per cent were traders assessed as individuals. The remainder, 249,591, were partners in 106,800 unincorporated firms. The average number of partners per firm was 2.34.[1] Information on this question has not hitherto been available. Stamp[2] discusses a number of attempts to estimate the total number of partners in firms, and the average number of partners per firm for years before 1914. He reports the results of a

---

[1] The totals in this paragraph, as in other sections of this Appendix, include the Finance group.
[2] *British Incomes and Property* (1916) pp. 244–7.

sample inquiry made by himself. The sample consisted of firms accounting for one-eleventh of the total number. From this sample, Stamp concluded that the average number of partners per firm was 2.4. This figure apparently refers to the years immediately before 1914. Bowley had used a multiplier of 2.5 in calculations made in 1906. Stamp was able to classify the firms in his sample by the size of the gross assessment made on each, and found a steady increase in the average number of partners per firm from 2.16 in the class assessed at £160–£400, to 3.75 in the class assessed at more than £10,000. Nearly 75 per cent of all the firms in the sample had 2 partners, 17 per cent had 3, and nearly 9 per cent had more than 3 partners. It is not possible to make similar calculations for the assessment year 1928–29. The close similarity of the average number of partners for all firms obtained by Stamp about 1913 and by us for 1928–29 may mask differences in the average numbers at different levels of assessment (and True Income). The distribution of firms among trade groups changed between 1913 and the late 1920's, and this might be expected to affect the average number of partners in *all* firms, in so far as the average number of partners per firm varied from trade group to trade group.

In the figures given for 1928–29 there does seem to be a marked consistency in the average number of partners for firms in different trade groups. With an overall average of 2.34 partners per firm in the U.K., 62 out of the 77 trade groups distinguished in Table E lie within the range of 2.25 to 2.55 partners per firm.

The distribution among the major branches of productive activity of the total number of individuals, firms, partners and 'entrepreneurial persons' associated with non-corporate concerns is shown in the following table.

	Individuals		Firms		Partners		'Entrepreneurial persons'	
	No.	%	No.	%	No.	%	No.	%
Extraction ..	2,002	0.3	672	0.6	1,748	0.7	3,750	0.3
Manufacturing ..	46,702	5.7	18,600	17.4	43,757	17.5	90,459	8.5
Distribution ..	564,350	69.3	59,800	56.0	136,480	54.7	700,830	65.9
Transport ..	23,065	2.8	4,609	4.3	11,349	4.6	34,414	3.2
Finance ..	17,685	2.2	2,890	2.7	7,470	3.0	25,155	2.4
Professions ..	84,796	10.4	14,739	13.8	34,721	13.9	119,517	11.2
Misc. Activities ..	76,113	9.3	5,490	5.2	14,066	5.6	90,179	8.5
Total	814,713	100	106,800	100	249,591	100	1,064,304	100

The distributive group accounted for nearly 70 per cent of the individual traders and nearly two-thirds of the 'entrepreneurial persons' associated with non-corporate concerns assessed in 1928-29. In absolute terms, 564,350 individuals and 136,480 partners were assessed in this group, making up a total of 700,830 'entrepreneurial persons' associated with non-corporate concerns mainly engaged in distribution. The average number of partners per firm in this group was 2.28, lower than that in any other major activity group. Concerns mainly engaged in *retail* distribution accounted for 86 per cent of the individuals, 87 per cent of the partners, and 89 per cent of the 'entrepreneurial persons' associated with non-corporate distributive concerns. The total number of 'entrepreneurial persons' in the retail section of the distributive group was 567,328. This number was about 53 per cent of the total number of 'entrepreneurial persons' associated with *all* non-corporate productive enterprises. The average number of partners per firm assessed in the retail trade group was 2.26. Amongst retail traders, rather more than half (55 per cent) of both the number of individual assessments and the total number of 'entrepreneurial persons' assessed were mainly engaged in retail distribution in the strict sense. The remainder consisted of retail distributors who also 'manufactured' some of the goods they distributed. This section included small bakers, bespoke tailors and shoe-makers. The remainder of the distributive group consisted of wholesale distributors and hotels, inns and similar concerns.

The professions, as defined for the present purpose, accounted for about 10 per cent of the individuals, 14 per cent of the partners and 11 per cent of the 'entrepreneurial persons' associated with non-corporate concerns assessed in 1928-29. Individuals assessed in the professional group numbered 84,796; partners in firms 34,721; and 'entrepreneurial persons' 119,517. The number of partners per firm was 2.36.

Apart from the residual group of undifferentiated 'other' professions the largest single group was medicine and dentistry. 32,673 'entrepreneurial persons' were covered by the assessments made in this group. Of these assessments, 25,096 or 77 per cent were made on individuals. The average number of partners per firm was 2.19, which was the lowest of any trade group in the U.K. The number of assessments made on 'Companies and Local Authorities etc.' in this group was negligible (59). Consequently the number of 'entrepreneurial persons' mainly engaged in medicine and dentistry may be taken to represent practically the whole number of persons practising medicine and dentistry on their own account in 1927. (Doctors and dentists employed by other undertakings, local authorities and the central government were not assessed under Schedule D.)

Law accounted for 17,275 'entrepreneurial persons', and accountancy for 10,566. The average number of partners per firm was rather higher in these groups than in most trade groups. The averages were 2.47 and 2.60 respectively in law and accountancy. The figures for these professions related only to persons practising on their own account and not to those employed by other concerns.

The only other clearly defined 'major branch of activity' that accounted for a significant proportion of 'entrepreneurial persons' was manufacturing industry. The industries in this group accounted for only 5.7 per cent of the total number of assessed *individuals* but included 8.5 per cent of the 'entrepreneurial persons' associated with non-corporate concerns. The difference is explained by the relatively large number of firms in the manufacturing group (17.4 per cent of the total number of firms assessed in 1928–29). Some 46,702 individuals, 43,757 partners and 90,459 'entrepreneurial persons' were assessed in 1928–29. In addition, a large number of partnerships mainly engaged in manufacturing industry were operating as private companies in 1928–29. Of the sub-groups of the manufacturing industries distinguished in the main tables of this report, the miscellaneous manufacturing group contained the largest number of 'entrepreneurial persons' (31,075). The second largest group was the building trades (including brick and cement manufacture and the timber trades). This group included 25,601 'entrepreneurial persons' associated with non-corporate enterprises, this number being almost equally divided between individual traders and partners. The average number of partners per firm in this group was 2.36. The concerns mainly engaged in building and contracting included 18,327 'entrepreneurial persons', of whom rather more than half were partners, and 9,053 individual traders.

No non-corporate concern was engaged in railway transport in 1928–29. Practically all the individuals, firms and associated 'entrepreneurial persons' assessed in the transport group were mainly engaged in road transport of passengers or frieght. 22,059 individuals, 10,149 partners and 32,208 'entrepreneurial persons' were covered by the non-corporate assessments made on these concerns in 1928–29.

Of the definite trade groups distinguished in the main tables of this report, each of the following accounted for more than 10,000 'entrepreneurial persons' associated with non-corporate enterprise in 1928–29:

		persons
Retail (purely distributive)	... ...	307,280
Retail (semi-industrial) ...	... ...	260,048
Hotels, Inns, etc.	... ...	77,061
Wholesale distribution ...	... ...	56,441
Medicine and Dentistry ...	... ...	32,673
Road Transport	... ...	32,208
Building and Contracting	... ...	18,327
Brokers and Agents (other than stock-brokers)	...	12,675
Accountancy ...	... ...	10,566

Together these trade groups accounted for 75 per cent of the total number of 'entrepreneurial persons' assessed in non-corporate concerns in 1928–29.

The number of 'entrepreneurial persons' may be related to the Gross True Income assessed on non-corporate enterprises. As explained in the body of the report, the number of assessments and the True Income assessed are not strictly comparable. Moreover the crude average True Income per 'entrepreneurial person' is a somewhat artificial statistic, in view of the wide dispersion of the True Income assessed in each trade group. Nevertheless, the averages are of some interest. From some points of view they are more meaningful than the figures for average True Income per *assessment* given in the Main Tables.

The average Gross True Income per 'entrepreneurial person' in all non-corporate concerns assessed in 1928–29 was £380. There were of course considerable differences in this average between the various trade groups, and the overall figure is heavily weighted downwards by the preponderance of low-earning concerns in distribution. The averages for the major branches of activity were as follows, arranged in order of size.

		£
Finance	... ...	1,060
Professions	... ...	610
Manufacturing	... ...	580
Extraction	... ...	510
Transport	... ...	340
Distribution	... ...	320
Miscellaneous	... ...	140

Among the main sections of the manufacturing industries, the averages were as follows:

				£
Textiles	...	...	...	1,000
Chemicals	...	...	...	880
Food, Drink and Tobacco		...		660
Other Manufacturing		...	...	580
Building	...	...	...	560
Metals	...	...	...	450
Public Utilities	...	...	...	160

In concerns operating overseas, the average Gross True Income per entrepreneurial person was £520. The number of such persons in this group was only 1,312, made up of 1,076 individuals and 236 partners in 83 firms. Over 60 per cent of these persons were engaged in the unclassified activities designated 'Other Concerns'. The majority of the remainder were occupied in Land or Plantations.

TABLE E
Number of Original Assessments on Non-corporate Enterprises in 1928–29 (1927)

	In-dividuals (1)	Firms (2)	Partners (3)	Persons (1)+(3) (4)	Partners per firm (5)
Coal Mines	275	230	642	917	2.79
Iron Mines ..	17	8	18	35	2.25
Other Mines	42	15	34	76	2.27
Quarries	1,668	419	1,054	2,722	2.52
EXTRACTION	*2,002*	*672*	*1,748*	*3,750*	*2.60*
Cotton	230	166	428	658	2.58
Wool	512	363	904	1,416	2.49
Silk	156	86	195	351	2.27
Flax, Jute, Hemp	469	175	428	897	2.45
Lace	214	87	209	423	2.40
Hosiery	281	206	512	793	2.49
Misc. Textiles	192	90	209	401	2.32
Bleaching and Dyeing	199	123	311	510	2.53
TEXTILES	*2,253*	*1,296*	*3,196*	*5,449*	*2.47*
Iron and Steel	411	272	677	1,088	2.49
Machinery and Engineering	2,976	1,461	3,390	6,366	2.32
Shipbuilding	331	179	442	773	2.47
Rly. Carriage and Wagon	34	14	33	67	2.36
Motor and Cycle	966	452	1,027	1,993	2.27
Anchor, Chain, etc. ..	203	86	206	409	2.40
Small Arms, Tools, etc.	1,473	450	1,025	2,498	2.28
Wrought Iron and Steel Tube	711	383	911	1,622	2.38
Copper and Brass	523	265	624	1,147	2.35
Gold and Silver Plate	1,068	389	878	1,946	2.26
Lead, Tin, Zinc	69	40	97	166	2.43
Tinplate	112	47	109	221	2.32
Misc. Metals	257	132	308	565	2.33
METALS	*9,134*	*4,170*	*9,727*	*18,861*	*2.33*

	In-dividuals (1)	Firms (2)	Partners (3)	Persons (1)+(3) (4)	Partners per firm (5)
Grain Milling	1,277	346	808	2,085	2.34
Biscuit and Bread	153	59	147	300	2.49
Sugar and Glucose	79	27	64	143	2.37
Cocoa and Confectionery	288	142	333	621	2.35
Misc. Foods	688	285	716	1,404	2.51
Brewing	460	217	529	989	2.44
Distilling	13	10	26	39	2.60
Mineral Waters	514	166	410	915	2.42
Tobacco	94	39	93	187	2.38
FOOD, DRINK AND TOBACCO	*3,566*	*1,291*	*3,117*	*6,683*	*2.41*
Fine Chemicals	326	113	254	580	2.25
Patent Medicines	58	11	69	127	6.27
Soap and Candles	93	32	76	169	2.38
Fertilizers, Explosives, etc.	572	247	607	1,179	2.46
CHEMICALS	*1,049*	*403*	*1,006*	*2,055*	*2.50*
Leather and Rubber	1,286	482	1,129	2,415	2.34
Boots and Shoes	1,240	399	940	2,180	2.36
Misc. Clothing	4,872	1,477	3,348	8,220	2.27
Paper-making	124	63	161	285	2.56
Printing and Bookbinding	4,267	1,390	3,185	7,452	2.29
Publishing, Newspapers	449	204	495	944	2.43
Stationery	651	252	587	1,238	2.33
Furniture	2,063	639	1,479	3,542	2.31
Pottery, China, etc.	148	103	260	408	2.52
Glass	170	75	184	354	2.45
Instruments	1,646	510	1,155	2,801	2.26
Manufactures n.e.s.	628	261	608	1,236	2.33
OTHER MANUFACTURING	*17,544*	*5,855*	*13,531*	*31,075*	*2.33*
Building and Contracting	9,053	3,957	9,274	18,327	2.34
Bricks, cement, etc.	645	359	904	1,549	2.52
Timber	2,938	1,184	2,787	5,725	2.35
BUILDING	*12,636*	*5,500*	*12,965*	*25,601*	*2.36*
Gas	45	17	54	99	3.18
Water	347	20	52	399	2.60
Electricity	128	48	109	237	2.27
PUBLIC UTILITIES	*520*	*85*	*215*	*735*	*2.53*
MANUFACTURING	*46,702*	*18,600*	*43,757*	*90,459*	*2.35*
Wholesale Dist.	35,772	8,745	20,669	56,441	2.36
Hotels, Inns, etc.	71,408	2,416	5,653	77,061	2.34
Retail (purely distributive)	253,610	23,569	53,670	307,280	2.28
Retail (semi-industrial)	203,560	25,070	56,488	260,048	2.25
DISTRIBUTION	*564,350*	*59,800*	*136,480*	*700,830*	*2.28*
Docks, Canals	121	21	51	172	2.43
Shipping	654	251	875	1,529	3.49
Ships' managers	231	107	274	505	2.56
Road Transport	22,059	4,230	10,149	32,208	2.40
TRANSPORT	*23,065*	*4,609*	*11,349*	*34,414*	*2.46*

	In-dividuals (1)	Firms (2)	Partners (3)	Persons (1)+(3) (4)	Partners per firm (5)
British Banks	15	22	92	107	4.18
Insurance	4,713	244	577	5,290	2.36
Stockbrokers and Jobbers	1,414	1,062	3,097	4,511	2.92
Finance houses, Bill-brokers	2,135	175	437	2,572	2.50
Other brokers and agents	9,408	1,387	3,267	12,675	2.36
FINANCE	*17,685*	*2,890*	*7,470*	*25,155*	*2.58*
Law	8,129	3,701	9,146	17,275	2.47
Medicine and Dentistry	25,096	3,456	7,577	32,673	2.19
Literature and Art	7,198	173	404	7,602	2.34
Music and Drama	7,447	130	297	7,744	2.28
Accountancy	5,456	1,962	5,110	10,566	2.60
Eng., Arch.	6,346	1,394	3,158	9,504	2.27
Other Professions	25,124	3,923	9,029	34,153	2.30
PROFESSIONS	*84,796*	*14,739*	*34,721*	*119,517*	*2.36*
MISC. SERVICES	*76,113*	*5,490*	*14,066*	*90,179*	*2.56*
ALL PRODUCTIVE ACTIVITIES	*814,713*	*106,800*	*249,591*	*1,064,304*	*2.34*
Railways O.U.K.	—	3	6	6	2.00
Cables, Telegraphs	34	2	4	38	2.00
Mineral Properties	27	4	11	38	2.75
Oil Concessions	1	—	—	1	—
Public Utilities	22	2	4	26	2.00
Land and Mortgage	88	15	44	132	2.93
Plantations	138	30	105	243	3.50
Banks	11	1	2	13	2.00
Other Concerns	755	26	60	815	2.31
Adventures O.U.K.	*1,076*	*83*	*236*	*1,312*	*2.84*